SCHOLASTIC
LITERACY SKILLS

Handwriting
Years 5–6

TERMS AND CONDITIONS

IMPORTANT – PERMITTED USE AND WARNINGS – READ CAREFULLY BEFORE USING

Copyright in the software contained in this CD-ROM and in its accompanying material belongs to Scholastic Limited. All rights reserved. © 2013 Scholastic Ltd.

Save for these purposes, or as expressly authorised in the accompanying materials, the software may not be copied, reproduced, used, sold, licensed, transferred, exchanged, hired, or exported in whole or in part or in any manner or form without the prior written consent of Scholastic Ltd. Any such unauthorised use or activities are prohibited and may give rise to civil liabilities and criminal prosecutions.

The material contained on this CD-ROM may only be used in the context for which it was intended in *Scholastic Literacy Skills*, and is for use only in the school which has purchased the book and CD-ROM, or by the teacher who has purchased the book and CD-ROM. Permission to download images is given for purchasers only and not for users from any lending service. Any further use of the material contravenes Scholastic Ltd's copyright and that of other rights holders.

This CD-ROM has been tested for viruses at all stages of its production. However, we recommend that you run virus-checking software on your computer systems at all times. Scholastic Ltd cannot accept any responsibility for any loss, disruption or damage to your data or your computer system that may occur as a result of using either the CD-ROM or the data held on it.

IF YOU ACCEPT THE ABOVE CONDITIONS YOU MAY PROCEED TO USE THE CD-ROM.

Minimum system requirements:

- Windows: XP (Service Pack 3), Vista (Service Pack 2) or Windows 7 with 2.33GHz processor
- Mac: OS 10.6 to 10.7 with Intel Core™ Duo processor
- 1GB RAM (recommended)
- 1024 x 768 Screen resolution
- CD-ROM drive (24x speed recommended)
- 16-bit sound card
- Adobe Reader 9.3.4

For all technical support queries, please phone Scholastic Customer Services on 0845 6039091.

SCHOLASTIC

Book End, Range Road, Witney, Oxfordshire,
OX29 0YD

www.scholastic.co.uk

© 2013, Scholastic Ltd

123456789 3456789012

British Library Cataloguing-in-Publication Data
A catalogue record for this book is available
from the British Library.

ISBN 978-1407-12789-7
Printed by Bell & Bain Ltd, Glasgow

All rights reserved. This book is sold subject to the condition that it shall not, by way of trade or otherwise, be lent, hired out or otherwise circulated without the publisher's prior consent in any form of binding or cover other than that in which it is published and without a similar condition, including this condition, being imposed upon the subsequent purchaser.

No part of this publication may be reproduced, stored in a retrieval system, or transmitted, in any form or by any means, electronic, mechanical, photocopying, recording or otherwise, other than for the purposes described in the lessons in this book, without the prior permission of the publisher. This book remains in copyright, although permission is granted to copy pages where indicated for classroom distribution and use only in the school which has purchased the book, or by the teacher who has purchased the book, and in accordance with the CLA licensing agreement. Photocopying permission is given
only for purchasers and not for borrowers of books from any lending service.

Due to the nature of the web we cannot guarantee the content or links of any site mentioned. We strongly recommend that teachers check websites before using them in the classroom.

Author
Gillian Howell

Series consultant
Amanda McLeod

Editorial
Rachel Mackinnon, Melissa Rugless,
Vicky Butt, Jennie Clifford

Series Designers
Shelley Best and Anna Oliwa

Designer
Andrea Lewis

Illustrations
Mark Brierley/Beehive Illustration

Every effort has been made to trace copyright holders for the works reproduced in this book, and the publishers apologise for any inadvertent omissions.

Scholastic Literacy Skills
Handwriting: Years 5–6

Contents

- INTRODUCTION 4
- SERIES OVERVIEW 6
- USING THE BOOK 8
- HOW TO USE THE CD-ROM 9
- RIGHT-HANDED WRITERS 10
- LEFT-HANDED WRITERS 12
- JOINING 14

Chapter 1
Revision of the joins

- INTRODUCTION 15
- END-LOW DIAGONAL JOINS 16
- END-LOW DROP-ON JOINS 20
- END-HIGH HORIZONTAL JOINS 24
- END-HIGH DIAGONAL JOINS 28
- END-HIGH DROP-ON JOINS 32
- END-HIGH TO 'e' JOINS 36
- TRICKY JOINS 40

Chapter 2
Suffixes

- INTRODUCTION 44
- ADDING A SUFFIX 45
- TRANSFORMING NOUNS TO VERBS 49
- TRANSFORMING VERBS TO NOUNS 53
- COMPARATIVES 57
- OTHER SUFFIXES 61

Chapter 3
Prefixes and word roots

- INTRODUCTION 65
- PREFIX REVISION 66
- PREFIXES FOR NEGATION (1) 70
- PREFIXES FOR NEGATION (2) 74
- WORDS WITH A LATIN ROOT (1) 78
- WORDS WITH A LATIN ROOT (2) 82

Chapter 4
Common letter strings

- INTRODUCTION 86
- DIFFERENT SPELLING, SAME SOUND 87
- THE LETTER 'c' 91
- CONNECTIVES 95
- SAME SPELLING, DIFFERENT SOUND .. 99
- WORD FAMILIES 103

Chapter 5
Refining handwriting

- INTRODUCTION 107
- CHANGING THE SIZE 108
- DEVELOPING YOUR OWN STYLE 112
- PUNCTUATION 116
- PRACTISING SPEED 120
- WRITING TASKS 124

Introduction

About the series

Even in today's computer world, handwriting remains an essential literacy skill. Without effortless script, children may find it difficult to reach their academic potential; and poor presentation can affect grades. A person with good handwriting does not need to concentrate on the formation of letters and words. The result will be a fast, legible script that is easy for others to read. Effortless handwriting allows a writer to concentrate on structure, content, clarity, consistency, varied vocabulary, grammar and spelling.

This series aims to help children develop a clear, fluent, legible and fast handwriting style by giving them the opportunity to acquire this in their first year of school, or when entering the school at a later stage. It is, however, also for older children who have difficulties with particular areas of handwriting.

Learning to write is not just about memorising patterns and this series progresses through:
- Motor and visual perception skills.
- Alphabet (lower-case and capitals) and numbers.
- Learning to join.
- Establishing and reinforcing secure joining through spelling work.
- Developing speed, fluency, individualisation and presentation skills.

In many handwriting schemes, the needs of left-handed students are mostly ignored, or only briefly touched upon. In this series, left-handers' needs are addressed throughout, with tips on classroom organisation and practical support. Many left-handers find it more difficult to form rounded letters and therefore a slightly more italic-style script is often more suitable. We show how this alternative script can be taught to left-handers and make suggestions about how to teach both left- and right-handers, together, during group sessions. Specifics for left-handers are included in each teachers' notes section.

In this three-book series children will be taught to:
- Recognise the importance of producing clear and neat work in order to communicate successfully.
- Take pride in their presentation and equate handwriting with a sense of achievement.
- Write quickly in order to express themselves fluently on paper.
- Use their skills with confidence in everyday life.
- Achieve a high standard of penmanship.

Handwriting policies

Purposeful handwriting is a vital part of learning to write. Schools, however, should still have a separate handwriting policy to ensure a consistent approach to handwriting throughout the school. It should include:
- Your aims
- Terminology
- Organisation for each year
- Time allocation for each year
- Planning, assessment, record-keeping, marking, feedback strategies
- Development plans
- Classroom set-up
- Posture
- Pencil grip
- Writing implements
- Left- and right-handed support
- SEN and Gifted and Talented provision
- Cross-curricular links
- Subject coordinators', teachers' and teaching assistants' roles
- Health and safety
- Equal opportunities
- References.

Treat your handwriting policy sensibly. Children starting school after Reception may already be writing. Assess their work. If letter formation is correct, children shouldn't learn another style. Children forced to learn alternative styles can get confused resulting in a merged incorrect script, which can be laboured and illegible.

Your policy should also include the key things you should be aiming for the children to learn:
- To hold a pen or pencil with an appropriate grip.
- To form upper- and lower-case letters correctly.
- To write on a page from left to right, and from top to bottom.
- To form letters in a consistent size and shape.
- To space letters and words appropriately.
- To join letters.
- To present work clearly and legibly so their work can be easily read.

Classroom set-up
Organising the classroom correctly is important. In an ideal room, there should be several tables and chairs of various heights to meet the needs of the shortest to the tallest in the class (see 'Posture', page 10). Swap some of your furniture with the years below, and above, to facilitate this. Sit left-handers to the left of right-handers, or next to another left-hander. This will ensure that their elbows don't bump together. Reposition children if overhead lights throw a shadow over their work. Children should also be able to look at the board without having to crane their heads awkwardly.

Raised writing surfaces
Raised writing surface easels, enabling children to see their writing more easily, are helpful for those who need to reduce writing strain (resulting from a tremor or poor posture) or to help correct a hook-hand position, as children can see their writing more easily. These will force children to sit more upright with their eyes about 30cm from the paper. If your school does not have any manufactured writing easels, you can easily make one by using a semi-full A4 lever-arch file and turning it horizontally towards the front of the desk. The best angle will vary for each child but 20 degrees is a good starting point. Add or remove paper to raise or lower the angle.

Writing equipment
Individual whiteboards and whiteboard pens should be available for all children across the key stages. These give children the opportunity to practise without leaving an indelible mark, helping to build the confidence of the reluctant writer. However, be careful about their posture when using them.

Many children do not like the typical HB fat pencil they may be given to use in Reception to Year 2 classes. These can promote a tight-fisted heavy-handed grip. Instead, a range of fat, thin, round, hexagonal and triangular pencils with soft, medium and hard leads should be available for children to experiment with during their early writing years. A softer B lead can be used to encourage lighter pressure. This is particularly useful for left-handers who want to speed up. Pencil grips should also be provided for colouring pencils.

Pens should be provided for Key Stage 2 children. Liquid ink pens, although more expensive than ballpoints, promote a lighter hand as less pressure needs to be applied to the pen to produce a clean line. This reduces stress on the hand while writing, which saves energy, promotes comfort and results in faster writing.

If fountain pens are preferred, it is important to provide left- and right-handed pens (left-handed nibs curve slightly to the left allowing the child to pull, rather than push, across the page). Left-handers using a right-handed pen will find it will dig into the paper when being pushed across the page; the ink will not flow freely and will appear in blotches, slowing them down.

To introduce children to fountain pens, you should:
- Compare a full and empty ink cartridge. Find the ball at the bottom of the empty cartridge and find it at the entrance of the full one.
- Look inside the pen and find the punch that pushes the ball out of the top of the cartridge.
- See how the cartridge fits around the punch and encourage children to realise it is like a straw for ink to flow inside. Explain that ink is pulled out of the cartridge, through the 'straw', when the nib is pulled across page.
- Compare a pencil and ballpoint pen. The pencil and ballpoint can work in any position.
- Compare a calligraphy nib and modern fountain nib. Both nibs need to be held in the correct pen grip and flat against the paper. The calligraphy nib will only work with the correct pen hold, while the modern fountain nib is slightly more forgiving. If the children can feel the pen scratching when pulled across the paper, then it is in the wrong position. Many children don't realise this as the ink trace is still there.

Font
The font used in this scheme can be found on page 11. While the form of 'f' in this font may seem unusual, it means that the children do not have to relearn letter formation when they start to join. It is, however, important that children recognise the print 'f' and when to use it.

Note
Children should be made aware that handwriting should not hurt. If they experience on-going pain, they should draw this to your attention for further investigation.

Series overview

Reception–Year 2

Chapter	Coverage and focus	About
1: Motor skills	Gross motor skills and crossing the midline	Exercises and activities to help develop the skills needed for handwriting.
	Proprioception	
	Visual perception	
	Fine motor practical exercise	
	Fine motor paper exercise	
	General fine motor patterning exercises	
2: Patterning	Warm-up exercises	Activities to use before every handwriting lesson. Videos provided on the CD-ROM.
	Straight down shapes	Patterning exercises for the different letter shapes.
	Down, up and over shapes	
	Up, backwards and around shapes	
	Zooming shapes	
3: Introducing letters	Introducing the letter stories	Letter stories using the character 'Lenny Lizard' to demonstrate the letter shapes. Supported by animations for each lower-case letter on the CD-ROM.
	lower-case letters 's', 'a', 't', 'p', 'i', 'n', 'm', 'd', 'g', 'o', 'c', 'k', 'e', 'u', 'r', 'h', 'f', 'l', 'j', 'q', 'w', 'x', 'y', 'z'	Letters are introduced in phonic order, but sheets are flexible and could be used in a letter groups order. Supported by animations on the CD-ROM.
4: Capitals and numbers	Capitals A–Z	Capitals are introduced in alphabetical order. Supported by animations on the CD-ROM.
	Numbers 1–10	Numbers 1–10 are introduced. Supported by animations on the CD-ROM.
5: Joining	Alternative forms: 'e' and 's'	When joining, the letters 'e' and 's' often take a different form when in the middle of a word. This introduces the alternative style.
	End-low diagonal joins: 'ch', 'sh', 'th', 'qu', 'ck', 'ai', 'air', 'er', 'soft g''	Joins are introduced in one-by-one encouraging children to end the letter and continue to the start of the next letter. Supported by animations on the CD-ROM.
	End-low drop-on joins: 'ed', 'ng', 'ear', 'igh'	
	End-high horizontal joins: 'or', 'oi', 'ow'	
	End-high diagonal joins: 'wh', 'ot', 'rk'	
	End-high drop-on joins: 'oo', 'oa', 'wa'	
	End-high to 'e': 'oe', 're'	End-high to 'e' is an end-high drop-on join but is given its own section as it is a tricky join. Supported by animations on the CD-ROM.
	Tricky joins: 'ss', 'ff', 'ee', 'zz'	Other tricky joins: where a second-style of a letter is used, it is a difficult movement or an unusual letter combination. Supported by animations on the CD-ROM.

Years 3–4

Chapter	Coverage and focus	About
1: Revision of joins	End-low diagonal joins: words starting with 'a', words containing 'u' and 'i'	Revise the joins introduced in the Reception–Year 2 book. Supported by animations on the CD-ROM.
	End-low drop-on joins: 'ha', 'to', 'ba'	
	End-high horizontal joins: 'ri', 'wi', 'om'	
	End-high diagonal joins: 'ok', 'ot', 'rl'	
	End-high drop-on joins: 'ra', 'wo', 'og'	
	End-high to 'e': 'ure', 've', 'we'	
	Tricky joins: 'ss', 'ee', joins to/from 'x'	
2: Suffixes	Regular verb endings '-ed', '-ing', '-y'	Practise handwriting while covering key suffixes. Supported by animations on the CD-ROM.
	Noun endings: '-s', '-es', 'y' to '-ies'	
	Common suffixes (1): '-ly', '-less', '-ful'	
	Common suffixes (2): '-able', '-er', '-est'	
	Common suffixes (3): '-tion', '-ic', '-ist'	

Years 3–4 continued

Chapter	Coverage and focus	About
3: Prefixes	Prefixes (1): 'un-', 'dis-', 're-'	Practise handwriting while covering key prefixes. Supported by animations on the CD-ROM.
	Prefixes (2): 'pre-', 'de-', 'mis-'	
	Prefixes (3): 'micro-', 'mini-', 'auto-'	
	Prefixes (4): 'circ-', 'tele-', 'trans-'	
	Number prefixes: 'bi-', 'tri-', 'oct-'	
4: Common letter strings	'gh' letter strings: '-ough', '-igh', '-ight'	Practise handwriting while covering common letter stings. Supported by animations on the CD-ROM.
	Silent letters: 'kn-', '-mb', 'wr-'	
	Pronouns	
	Homophones	
	Contractions: n't, 're, 've, 'll, 'd	
5: Refining handwriting	Spot the errors	Examine examples of handwriting and to find errors and correct them.
	Change the size	Experiment with big and small writing for different purposes.
	Punctuation	Make sure children are able to use and position their punctuation correctly.
	Introducing speed and fluency	Practice writing quickly while maintaining legibility.
	Writing tasks	Longer writing activities to practise handwriting with.

Years 5–6

Chapter	Coverage and focus	About
1: Revision of joins	End-low diagonal joins: words starting with 'a', words containing 'u' and 'i'	Revise the joins previously covered. Supported by animations on the CD-ROM.
	End-low drop-on joins: 'ace', 'qua', 'af'	
	End-high horizontal joins: 'wn', 'vi', 'rm'	
	End-high diagonal joins: 'ob', 'rh', 'wl'	
	End-high drop-on joins: 'oc', 'rd', 'va'	
	End-high to 'e': 've', 're', 'oe'	
	Tricky joins: 'ss', 'ff', joins to/from 'x'	
2: Suffixes	Adding suffixes to words ending in 'e' or 'y': '-ing', '-est', '-ish', '-ment', '-ful', '-less'	Practise handwriting while covering key suffixes. Supported by animations on the CD-ROM.
	Transforming nouns to verbs: '-ate', '-en', '-ify'	
	Transforming verbs to nouns: '-ity', '-ism', '-ness'	
	Comparatives: '-er', '-est', '-like'	
	Other suffixes: '-ology', '-ance', '-ise'	
3: Prefixes	Prefix revision: 'un-', 'dis-', 'mis-'	Practise handwriting while covering key prefixes. Supported by animations on the CD-ROM.
	Prefixes for negation (1): 'il-', 'ir-', 'in-'	
	Prefixes for negation (2): 'im-', 'non-', 'anti-'	
	Words with a Latin root (1): 'prim-', 'aqua-', 'multi-'	
	Words with a Latin root (2): 'quad-', 'auto-', 'mari-'	
4: Common letter strings	Different spelling, same sound: '-cian', '-tion', '-sion'	Practise handwriting while covering common letter stings. Supported by animations on the CD-ROM.
	The letter 'c': 'ci', 'ce', 'cy', 'co', 'ca'	
	Connectives	
	Same spelling, different sound: 'ear', 'ie', 'ough'	
	Word families: 'ctu', 'tch', 'gue'	
5: Refining handwriting	Change the size	Experiment with big and small writing for different purposes.
	Developing your own style	Practise with different styles of writing.
	Punctuation	Make sure children are able to use and position their punctuation correctly.
	Practising speed	Practice writing quickly while maintaining legibility.
	Writing tasks	Longer writing activities to practise handwriting with.

Using the book

Before you conduct a handwriting lesson, remind yourself of good handwriting practice by referring to the information in the main introduction.

At the start of any new chapter, you should read the chapter introduction to get an overview of what is covered. The teachers' notes provide background knowledge along with an objective to share with the children. There will be a short paragraph about the accompanying photocopiable pages and how best to use them, as well as further ideas for practising handwriting in purposeful and fun ways.

Throughout the series, children will be guided in letter formation by Lenny Lizard. The terms 'head', 'body' and 'tail' will be used to describe letter size and there will be a visual prompt provided on most photocopiable pages.

How to structure a lesson

Handwriting lessons should be short 20–40 minute sessions. You can provide a focused and interactive session to engage children in the art of handwriting by combining the notes and photocopiable pages in this book with the CD-ROM provided.

- Begin your lesson with a fine or gross motor activity to get the children warmed up for a handwriting lesson. Such tasks could include pen-top walking; using putty or sticky tack to form shapes; using pegs as markers; coin sorting or solving a jigsaw puzzle.
- Have a whole-class session using the CD-ROM (see page 9).
- Identify the type of letter shape and join (if involved).
- Trace and/or write the letter, or spelling pattern, on the whiteboard ensuring you demonstrate best practice to the children.
- Encourage the children to join in by asking individuals to trace on the whiteboard. Get the whole class to skywrite, trace the letter shape on their legs or someone else's back.
- Then, use the photocopiable sheets and 'Further ideas' to reinforce your teaching when children move to their tables.

Writing sizes

The writing size varies between the books in the series as follows. The height refers to the body size (without ascenders or descenders).

- Reception–Year 2: individual letters 11mm and joining 8mm.
- Years 3–4: 5.5mm
- Years 5–6: 3.5mm

Children have different-sized writing. The height of the body letters that children form when writing their name is a good indication of what size their writing is. Letter size naturally changes so re-assess this termly (emotional trauma can also cause changes in size and style). The CD-ROM, therefore provides five sizes of lined paper for you to choose from (including a 2mm version). Rather than asking children to write on sheets that are the wrong size, provide them with our blank lined paper. Place the photocopiable sheet they need to complete by their side for them to copy from.

Home-school links

Send the 'Information for Parents' sheet (on the CD-ROM) home to help parents support their child at home. Ask parents to go over this with their child as it is important for children themselves to be aware of the practical elements needed for good handwriting along with an awareness of letter formation and size. You, also, should reinforce this during the course of the year (perhaps through children's drawings or making a class song). This encourages children to become aware of their posture, pencil grip, pencil and hand position.

How to use the CD-ROM

Below is brief guidance for using the CD-ROM. For more detailed information, see **How to use** on the main menu screen. The CD-ROM follows the structure of the book and contains:
- All of the photocopiable pages.
- Animations for all lower-case letters, capital letters, numbers and joins.
- Animations of the letter stories for lower-case letters.

Getting started
To begin using the CD-ROM, simply place it in your CD- or DVD-ROM drive. If the CD-ROM fails to auto-run, navigate to the drive and double-click on the red logo. You will then be given the option to install the program or to run it from the CD-ROM. By using the CD-ROM you are accepting our terms and conditions.

Main menu
The main menu screen is the first screen that appears. Here you can access: How to use the CD-ROM, credits and registration link. By clicking on any of the titled buttons you will be taken to the appropriate sub-menu. The **All photocopiables** button will provide a complete list of all the photocopiables within that CD-ROM.

Sub-menus
Below is a brief summary of what the sub-menus contain:

Letters and numbers
This section is a reference for how to form each individual divided into **Lower-case letters**, **Capitals** and **Numbers**. Within the sub-menu for lower-case letters, you can either navigate by **All letters** and select from an alphabetical list, or choose the appropriate letter-group. Each activity is structured in the same way: the first tab 'Introduction' provides an animation of the letter or number formation – use the playback buttons on-screen – and a practice area. The second tab 'Practice' provides space to practise using the whiteboard tools – trace over the grey letters or numbers or use the blank tramlines. The final tab 'Animation' provides the short animation for the relevant letter story.

Revision of joins
This sub-menu is structured in the same sequence as the revision chapter (see page 15). Each type of join leads to a further sub-menu with options for the relevant on-screen activities and links to the photocopiable sheets. Each activity includes an animation of the join formation and space to practise either on the blank tramlines, or by selecting an example from the word bank to trace over.

Suffixes
This sub-menu is divided into the same sections as the suffixes chapter (see page 44). Each section contains a further sub-menu with options for the relevant on-screen activities and links to the photocopiable sheets. Each activity includes an animation of the join formation and space to practise either on the blank tramlines, or by selecting an example word from the word bank to trace over.

Prefixes
This sub-menu is divided into the same sections as the prefixes chapter (see page 65). Each section contains a further sub-menu with options for the relevant on-screen activities and links to the photocopiable sheets. Each activity includes an animation of the join formation and space to practise either on the blank tramlines, or by selecting an example word from the word bank to trace over.

Common letter strings
This sub-menu is divided into the same sections as its related chapter (see page 86). Each section contains a further sub-menu with options for the relevant on-screen activities and links to the photocopiable sheets. Each activity includes a practice area and an introductory animation of the join formation, where applicable.

Refining handwriting
The sub-menu is structured in the same sequence as its related chapter (see page 107). Each section contains a further sub-menu with options for the relevant on-screen activities and links to the photocopiable sheets.

Whiteboard tools
The CD-ROM comes with its own set of whiteboard tools for use on any whiteboard. These include:
- Pen tool
- Eraser tool
- Three colours (black, blue, red).

Introduction

Right-handed writers

This information relates mainly to right-handers (see page 12 for left-handers).

Pencil grip
Many children start school with an established grip and early use of crayons and felt-tipped pens can encourage heavy pressure, an upright pen hold and unusual grip. We advocate a 'dynamic tripod' grip; while other grips may not hinder learning letter formation, they may hamper acquisition of speed and flow later. With good finger strength, the dynamic tripod grip allows the writer to manipulate fluidly, and speedily, around letter curves.

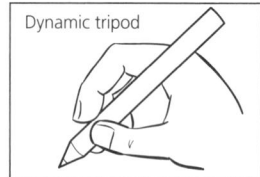

Some alternative grips (pictured below) that still allow for index and thumb manipulation are also suitable:

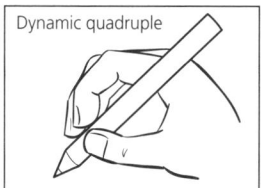

The dynamic quadruple grip is a more static grip but still may sometimes result in slower writing.

Pen held between index and middle fingers. This useful, alternative hold allows the pen to be held at any angle with little strain. Suggest it to children with handwriting difficulties resulting from an unconventional grip.

Whatever grip used, you should be aware of the child's whole hand. Check that their wrist does not rise, or twist; that their hand rests on their work, and is not too flattened or on its edge. These are an indication of weaker motor or visual perceptual skills, which may cause handwriting difficulties later.

The pencil end should point backwards over their shoulder in line with their forearm, not vertically upwards. Their hand should be positioned below the writing line so they can see their work without having to lean too far forwards.

Posture
Children with poor posture will find it difficult to reach the speeds they need and may suffer pain when writing. However, this may not be laziness but indicate an underlying visual problem, hypermobility or weakness in the core, shoulder or finger muscles. You will need to spot these indications and know when to refer to appropriate experts.

Both right- and left-handers should have the same sitting position:
- Feet – flat on the floor.
- Arms – resting on the forearms without the shoulders being forced upwards. Forearms should ideally be positioned 45 degrees to the table edge away from the body in order to support the shoulder girdle (approximately the same slant as the paper, see below).
- Back – should be almost straight (but slightly leaning forwards).
- Head – upright without the neck poking forwards.
- Weight – evenly distributed between feet and forearms.
- Non-writing hand – should support the work at the top corner furthest away from the writing hand. This allows the forearm to support the body enabling the writing arm to move lightly across the page. Children who support their work elsewhere on the page risk their supporting arm hindering their writing arm as they move down.

Paper position
Incorrect paper position makes it harder for the writer to see their work and encourages 'hooking' around above the writing line in order to see their letters. This 'hook' hinders the acquisition of fluid writing and speed.

Right-handers should position the paper towards their right side within their body range, not too far or too close. As they move down the page, they should move the paper up in the same line using their left hand, to maintain the correct body posture. The aim is to keep the right arm in the same position to avoid the elbow being cramped by the chest. It also prevents writing becoming cramped at the foot of the page.

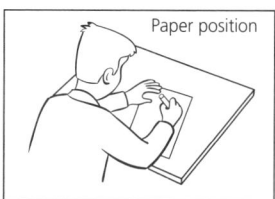
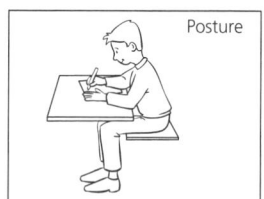

Introduction

Right-handed alphabet

a b c d e

f g h i j

k l m n o

p q r s t

u v w x y z

Introduction

Left-handed writers

Not all left-handers experience handwriting problems and, with correct teaching right from the very start, left-handedness shouldn't cause any problems. Without correct teaching, left-handers can easily adopt bad handwriting habits that cause illegibility, pain and hinder the acquisition of speed.

Most children at four years can tell which hand they prefer to write with but lateralisation dominance may not be established until eight or nine years. Encourage children to say which hand feels more comfortable to write with and place pencils straight in front of children's tummies to encourage them to choose. Look at their writing to see which letters look clearer and are better formed. Children who are forced into using the wrong hand experience difficulties with letter formation and may never attain the speeds they need later on. Children who haven't decided their lateralisation need to do motor skills and patterning work with both hands.

The following factors should be taken into account:
- Classroom set up (page 5).
- Writing implements (page 5).
- Pencil grip, posture, paper position (below).

Forming the letters
It is important to model writing with your left hand. Even if you are right-handed, and the result looks shaky, it will help you to understand the difficulties left-handers face, as well as demonstrate the correct formation for them.

This series advocates a flatter script for left-handers. For right-handers, the round curves of letters are easy as they pull their pen from left to right. A left-hander is expected to push across the page which is not an easy motion to achieve. A script such as that on page 13 will help to reduce the amount of pushing a left-hander has to do. It is italic in appearance, and the up, backwards and around shapes ('a', 'c', 'd', 'e', 'f', 'g', 'o' 'q' and 's') and down, up and over shapes ('b', 'h', 'k', 'm', 'n', 'p' and 'r') have flattened tops thus reducing the need to push across to form each letter. The thumb and index finger will have more of a pulling down motion and have a shorter distance to stretch around for curves and bumps.

Writing across the page
You should be aware that left-handers may display problems with directionality as they learn to write; mirrored letters are also quite common in the early years. Demonstrating and drawing attention to correct practice usually helps to clear these up unaided. If these problems persist in Year 2 and above, they may be an indication of dyslexia, dyspraxia or faulty eye convergence and you should refer to the appropriate expert.

Pencil grip
To help avoid a tight-fisted grip, left-handers should hold their pencil further away from the point than right-handers (about 2cm). Wrapping a rubber band around the pencil can help left-handers to judge this. They should take particular care to position their hand below the line they are writing on. This allows them to view their work, keep an upright body position and deters 'hooking' around their work.

To promote flow and speed, left-handers should move their hand and arm across the page while they form their letters; joining strokes are a good opportunity to do this.

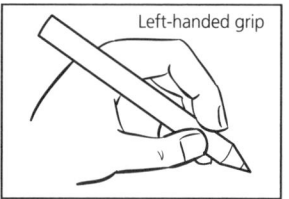
Left-handed grip

Posture
Left-handers should have the same posture as right-handers (see page 10). They may, however, wish to use a sloping board to raise their work slightly (see 'Raised writing surfaces' on page 5) or use a seat wedge to raise their bodies to allow them to see over their hand.

Paper position
Left-handers should position their paper towards the left side, within their body range, not too far or close to their body. As they move down the page while writing, they should use their right hand to move the paper up in the same line, to maintain the correct body posture and also prevent writing becoming cramped at the foot of the page. The aim is to keep the left arm in much the same position at all times to avoid the elbow being cramped by the chest.

Paper position

Introduction

Left-handed alphabet

a b c d e

f g h i j

k l m n o

p q r s t

u v w x y z

Introduction

Joining

The question of whether to join or write in a print script is controversial. However, anecdotal evidence reveals that children who join from Reception are less likely to revert to print when under exam pressure (and slow their writing speeds). Certainly, those who join write with fewer pen lifts and experience a greater flow across the paper leading to a faster and more mature script.

This series encourages children to join as soon as letter formation is established, however, it is vital not to teach children to join until their letter formation is completely correct. Incorrect formation hinders the acquisition of effortless joining and speed. It is therefore important to see a child's writing in action as, once written, it is very hard to tell whether an 'i' or 't' has been formed from the top or bottom (sometimes a darker mark can indicate the starting position but this is difficult to ascertain). Note, some children with weaker motor skills may not be able to join and all effort should be given towards building up motor strength before introducing joining.

Terminology
You may wish to develop your own terminology within the classroom to describe the movements involved in handwriting. However, there should be consistency and children should know the generic terms as they move from one year to the next. The following are universally applied to aid understanding as the child progresses from one year to the next: clockwise, anticlockwise, vertical, horizontal, diagonal, parallel, curve upwards, curve downwards, ascender, descender, letter, consonant, vowel, joined, sloped, top, middle, bottom, capital letter, small letter, upper-case letter and lower-case letter. Within this series, we refer to the handwriting guidelines (or tramlines) as head line, top body line, writing line and tail line.

Joining
Teach children that the concept of joining means moving their pencil, on the paper, from where one letter ends to the beginning of the next letter (or word space). To do this, teach children the important terms: 'end-low' and 'end-high' (see table).

Letter type	Letter sets	Explanation
End-low letters	'a' 'b' 'c' 'd' 'e' 'f' 'g' 'h' 'i' 'j' 'k' 'l' 'm' 'n' 'p' 'q' 's' 't' 'u' 'x' 'y' 'z'	All of these letters end with your pen on or below the baseline.
End-high letters	'o' 'r' 'v' 'w'	These letters end with your pen off the baseline.

Children find end-low joins easy; they simply travel up to where the next letter starts. Children who understand the concept of joining, also find end-high joins easy; they do not fall into the trap of coming back to the writing line before starting a new letter (as do children who write with entry strokes).

We have identified five main joins using the terms 'end-low' and 'end-high' with 'diagonal', 'drop-on' and 'horizontal' (see the table below).

Join type	Letters From	Letters To	Explanation
End-low diagonal joins	'a' 'b' 'c' 'd' 'e' 'f' 'g' 'h' 'i' 'j' 'k' 'l' 'm' 'n' 'p' 'q' 's' 't' 'u' 'x' 'y' 'z'	'b' 'h' 'i' 'j' 'k' 'l' 'm' 'n' 'p' 'r' 't' 'u' 'v' 'w' 'x' 'y' 'z'	When finishing on the writing line, or below, start the next by forming a diagonal join.
End-low drop-on joins	'a' 'b' 'c' 'd' 'e' 'f' 'g' 'h' 'i' 'j' 'k' 'l' 'm' 'n' 'p' 'q' 's' 't' 'u' 'x' 'y' 'z'	'a' 'c' 'd' 'e' 'f' 'g' 'o' 'q' 's'	When finishing on the writing line, or below, start the next by letting your pen go up and over. Then drop on to the start of the next letter before going backwards in the anticlockwise movement.
End-high horizontal joins	'o' 'r' 'v' 'w'	'i' 'j' 'm' 'n' 'p' 'r' 'u' 'v' 'w' 'x' 'y' 'z'	End-high horizontal joins go straight across to the start of the next letter.
End-high diagonal joins	'o' 'r' 'v' 'w'	'b' 'h' 'k' 'l' 't'	End-high diagonal joins only occur from end-high letters to ascenders. These joins curve upwards.
End-high drop-on joins	'o' 'r' 'v' 'w'	'a' 'c' 'd' 'e' 'f' 'g' 'o' 'q' 's'	End-high joins go straight across and drop on to the start of the next letter before going backwards in the anticlockwise movement. NOTE: End high to 'e' is a drop-on join but proves to be tricky so it is taught separately in this series.

Chapter 1
Revision of the joins

Introduction

This chapter focuses on revision of the joins that the children have learned in the previous books. Remember that joins should take you from the end of one letter to the beginning of the next. The joins are covered in the same sequence that the children encountered before (end-low diagonal, end-low drop-on, end-high horizontal, end-high diagonal, end-high drop-on, finishing with end-high to 'e' and tricky joins).

While specific joins are focused on in each section, there is also plenty of opportunity to practise a range of joins while doing the activities. When practising the joins, the children are also practising spelling, using words with common letter strings but different sounds and pronunciations. A variety of activities are used, including cloze passages, copying paragraphs and a poem, identifying rhyming words, arranging into alphabetical order, synonyms, definitions, letter writing, solving clues and riddles, wordsearches and writing inside shapes. Background knowledge about the joins is given at the start of each section for reference, as well as ideas for further activities to continue the children's practice.

It is important to demonstrate the correct letter and join formation. Remember to demonstrate with both your left and right hands and, when skywriting, to use mirror writing so the children see the letter as the correct shape.

In this chapter

End-low diagonal joins page 16	To practise writing words with the end-low diagonal join using words containing the vowels 'a', 'i' and 'u'.
End-low drop-on joins page 20	To practise writing words with the end-low drop-on join using words with the letter strings 'ace', 'qua' and 'af'.
End-high horizontal joins page 24	To practise writing words with the end-high horizontal join using words with the letter strings 'wn', 'vi' and 'rm'.
End-high diagonal joins page 28	To practise writing words with the end-high diagonal join using words with the letter strings 'ob', 'rh' and 'wl'.
End-high drop-on joins page 32	To practise writing words with the end-high drop-on join using words with the letter strings 'oc', 'rd' and 'va'.
End-high to 'e' joins page 36	To practise writing words with the end-high to 'e' join using words with the letter strings 've', 're' and 'oe'.
Tricky joins page 40	To practise tricky joins 'ss', 'ff' and 'x'.

End-low diagonal joins

Objective

To practise writing words with the end-low diagonal join using words containing the vowels 'a', 'i' and 'u'.

Background knowledge

This is the most common form of join. Children simply travel from where the letter ends on the writing line up to where the next letter begins.

Left-handers may wish to lift their pen from the paper while joining, thus avoiding having to push awkwardly across the page. If the ink or pencil trace disappears, do not tell them they have to produce a joining mark. However, do ensure they are joining just above the paper, rather than printing. Left-handers may also want to produce a sharper, more italic-style exit to their end-low joins. This is fine as long as they leave enough space between their words and don't cramp their letters together.

The words children practise during the activities focus on writing words with common letter strings but different pronunciations.

Activities

● **Photocopiable page 17 'Missing words'**
Children select a word from the choices provided to complete a sentence and write the correct word into a space in the sentence. The words all begin with the letter 'a' and use the end-low diagonal join, but have different pronunciations. Encourage the children to say the words aloud to explore the different 'a' vowel sounds. They practise the join further by identifying which two words share the same vowel sound and then make up a sentence that uses the remaining three words.

● **Photocopiable page 18 'Ouch!'**
This photocopiable sheet focuses on words containing 'u'. The children copy a short paragraph, enabling them to further practise the end-low diagonal join – 'thumb', 'built', 'unit' and 'jump' – as well as other joins. They then write their own sentence for each of the four words. Ask the children to read their new sentences aloud, and say the words aloud, to identify which of the four have the same vowel sound.

● **Photocopiable page 19 'Silent letters'**
Six words containing the letter 'i' are given (knit, ink, milk, bill, limb, finger). The children practise the end-low diagonal join by copying the words and putting them into alphabetical order. Two of the words, 'knit' and 'limb', contain silent letters. They identify these two words and write them again.

Further ideas

● **Coloured display:** Encourage the children to write their sentences on a piece of paper using a different colour crayon for each sentence. Use these as a handwriting display.
● **Writing implements:** Ask the children to write the same words or sentences on different types of surface using different writing implements, for example a blackboard and chalk, a whiteboard, paper and pencil, wax crayon and pen. Talk about the different effects and which is easier, faster or more attractive.
● **Comparison:** Ask one child to dictate a letter or short paragraph while their partner writes, then swap. Each then reads the other's writing and compares the result.

What's on the CD-ROM

On the CD-ROM you will find:
● Animation of the joins.
● All of the photocopiable pages.

Chapter 1

End-low diagonal joins

Missing words

■ Which word makes sense in these sentences? Choose a word, say it aloud and then write it in the space.

| aim | ant | aunt | autumn | album |

1. He took .... carefully before firing the arrow straight at the target.

2. The leaves turn into beautiful colours during ....

3. We made a lovely .... for our holiday photos.

4. My .... is coming to stay for two weeks.

5. I was bitten by a red .... in the garden.

■ Which two words begin with the same 'a' sound? Write them on the line below.

■ Write a sentence that uses the other three words.

PHOTOCOPIABLE

Scholastic Literacy Skills
Handwriting: Years 5–6   17

Chapter 1 Name:

End-low diagonal joins

Ouch!

■ Copy this paragraph. Pay particular attention to the words in bold.

When my mum **built** a new kitchen **unit**, she hit her **thumb** with a hammer. She yelled so loudly it made me **jump**!

■ Now write a new sentence for each word.

1. thumb

2. built

3. unit

4. jump

■ Read your sentences aloud and listen to the different vowel sounds in each word. Of the four words above, which two words have the same sound? Write them below.

Scholastic Literacy Skills
Handwriting: Years 5–6

PHOTOCOPIABLE
www.scholastic.co.uk

End-low diagonal joins

Name: Chapter 1

Silent letters

■ Write a label to name each of these pictures. Use the words below.

> ~~knit~~   bill   finger   ink   milk   limb

 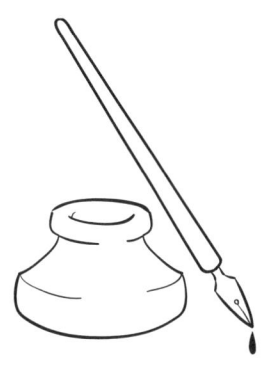 

knit

  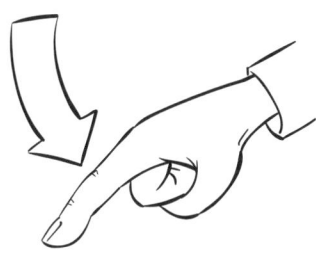

■ Now write the words in alphabetical order.

■ Which words have silent letters? Write them below.

Chapter 1

End-low drop-on joins

Objective

To practise writing words with the end-low drop-on join using words with the letter strings 'ace', 'qua', and 'af'.

Background knowledge

The drop-on join needs explicit teaching. Remind the children that the join takes them to where the next letter starts. In this case, the start of the drop-on letter is over at 1 o'clock, not 12 o'clock. This formation avoids gaps in the top of the letter. Teach children to end low, go up, go over and drop on to the start of the letter.

When forming the join, remind children to finish the letter first before travelling from the end of the letter to the start of the next. This will avoid the letters sitting on top of each other. Descender letters should be treated in exactly the same way.

Left-handers may wish to lift their pen from the paper while joining, thus avoiding having to push awkwardly across the page. If the ink or pencil trace disappears, do not tell them they have to produce a joining mark. However, do ensure they are joining just above the paper, rather than printing. Left-handers may also want to produce a sharper, more italic-style exit to their end-low joins. This is fine as long as they leave enough space between their words and don't cramp their letters together.

Activities

● **Photocopiable page 21 'Race day'**
The children practise the end-low drop-on join by copying a poem. Each line of the poem ends with a word containing the letter string 'ace'. They then further practise the words by identifying the rhymes and rewriting the rhyming words. The letters 'a' and 'c' are both drop-on letters.

● **Photocopiable page 22 'Synonyms'**
In this activity, children practise the end-low drop-on join with words containing medial 'q' and the letter string 'qua'. They are given five words and are asked to choose a word with a similar meaning from a word bank. They then write each pair of words next to each other. Children who are unsure of the meanings can use a dictionary to check their answers. They then use each word in a sentence of their own. The letters 'q' and 'a' are both drop-on letters.

● **Photocopiable page 23 'Complaint'**
A letter of complaint to a cafe about a missing raft provides the stimulus for this activity. The letter contains words with the end-low drop-on join in words using the 'af' letter string. The children then practise using the join by writing a reply from the cafe, ensuring they reuse the 'af' words: 'after', 'cafe', 'raft' and 'safe'. Discuss what form a letter in response might take, and ask the children to share their ideas orally with a partner before writing the letter. The letters 'a' and 'f' are both drop-on letters. Ensure the children do not add an extra cross to the letter 'f' as the descender join replaces it.

Further ideas

● **Poetry:** The children can copy their favourite poems using joined handwriting and decorate the edges as a frame for the poem. Use these as a class display.
● **Complaint:** Ask the children to choose an issue and compose a letter of complaint using joined handwriting. They could then swap with a partner and each write a response to their partner's complaint.

 What's on the CD-ROM

On the CD-ROM you will find:
● Animation of the joins.
● All of the photocopiable pages.

Scholastic Literacy Skills
Handwriting: Years 5–6

End-low drop-on joins

Race day

- Read the poem.
- Underline all the rhyming words.

>I really think it's ace
>That we are having a race
>I'll do up my shoelace
>And then I'll set the pace
>I'm in the lead by a great big space
>I win – a big smile on my face.
>Races are really ace!

- Write the rhyming words on the line below.

- What is the letter string they all share?

- Copy the poem below.

Chapter 1 Name:

End-low drop-on joins

Synonyms

■ Draw a line to match words with the same meaning.

water	quarrel
same	aqua
compress	squad
team	equal
argument	squash

■ Write the words in pairs below.

■ Write a sentence of your own using each of the words.

1. quarrel

2. aqua

3. squad

4. equal

5. squash

Name:　　　　　　　　　　　　　　　　　　　　　　Chapter 1

End-low drop-on joins

Complaint

■ Read the letter and write a response from the cafe owner. Make sure you use these words in your letter – 'after', 'cafe', 'raft', 'safe'.

To the Riverside Cafe

Dear Sir
I came to your cafe yesterday with a friend. We had been sailing our raft on the river and thought a cold drink would be good. We tied up the raft to the river bank and sat inside the cafe. After ten minutes, we left and found the raft had gone! We had tied it well and were sure it would be safe.
I am very sad that we have lost our raft and hope you might be able to help us find it.

Yours faithfully
Sailor Sam

Dear Sailor Sam

Chapter 1

End-high horizontal joins

Objective

To practise writing words with the end-high horizontal join using words with the letter strings 'wn', 'vi' and 'rm'.

Background knowledge

The end-high join to the letters 'i', 'j', 'm', 'n', 'p', 'r', 'u', 'v', 'w', 'x', 'y' and 'z' needs careful teaching. Remind children that the join takes them to where the next letter starts. In this case, the start of these is at the top of each letter. Going straight across avoids descending loopy joins that hinder legibility.

Teach children to end high and go straight across to the start of the letter. Remind them to finish the letter first before travelling from the end of the letter to the start of the next. This will avoid the letters sitting on top of each other.

Left-handers may wish to lift their pen from the paper while joining, thus avoiding having to push awkwardly across the page. If the ink or pencil trace disappears, do not tell them they have to produce a joining mark. However, do ensure they are joining just above the paper, rather than printing.

Activities

- **Photocopiable page 25 'Riddles'**
Four riddles are provided for the children to answer. All the answers contain 'wn', which uses the end-high horizontal join. (Answers for the first part are: 1 town, 2 yawn, 3 brown, 4 clown.) They then practise the join further by sorting the words into different word classes (nouns: town, yawn, clown; verbs: yawn, brown, clown; adjectives: brown; more than one word class: yawn, brown, clown). To help the children sort the words accurately, ask them to use each one in a phrase or sentence orally before writing.

- **Photocopiable page 26 'Civil wordsearch'**
The children have to find four words with the 'vi' letter string in a wordsearch and highlight, circle or underline each word. They practise using the end-high horizontal join by writing the words. A clue is given to help any children who struggle to find the words. The words are: civil, movie, view, vine.

- **Photocopiable page 27 'From 'arm' to 'worm''**
In this activity, the children follow instructions to change letters so that they change the word 'arm' into 'worm' in five stages. In the process, they practise the end-high horizontal join four times (arm, farm, firm, term, worm). They also have the opportunity to revise their alphabetical knowledge as the instructions focus on the alphabetical order of consonants and vowels. In order to make this part of the activity more challenging, you could mask the consonant/vowel guide before they begin.

Further ideas

- **Riddling:** Encourage the children to write their own riddles with the answer on the reverse. Display the collections and challenge children to see if they can answer them without cheating!
- **Word chain:** Provide the children with a four-letter word. Ask them to write it down and form a word chain by changing one letter at a time, for example: farm/harm/hare/dare/dark/park/pork and so on. Limit the time allowed for the activity, and compare the results. How different are the word chains? How many words are in the chains? Has the handwriting style remained consistent?

What's on the CD-ROM

On the CD-ROM you will find:
- Animation of the joins.
- All of the photocopiable pages.

Scholastic Literacy Skills
Handwriting: Years 5–6

Name: Chapter 1

End-high horizontal joins

Riddles

■ Solve the riddles to find the words containing the 'wn' spelling.

1. I am a place where people live and work but I am not a city or a village.

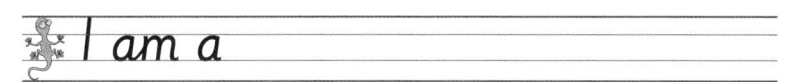

   I am a

2. If you see me doing this, you might do it too. I do it when I am tired and sometimes when I am bored.

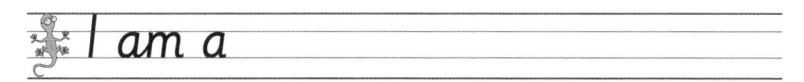

   I am a

3. I am not part of a rainbow, but I am a colour sometimes called tan.

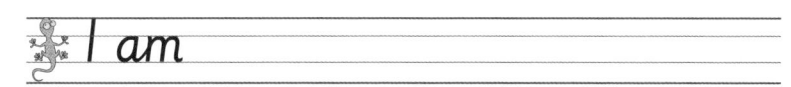

   I am

4. I make some people laugh, but some people don't like me at all.

   I am a

■ Write the riddle answers into the correct word class. Which words can belong to more than one class?

noun	
verb	
adjective	
more than one word class	

PHOTOCOPIABLE

Scholastic Literacy Skills
Handwriting: Years 5–6   25

Chapter 1   Name:

End-high horizontal joins

Civil wordsearch

■ Hidden in the wordsearch are four words with the letter string 'vi' in them. Can you find them?
■ Highlight, circle or underline each word.
■ There is a clue at the bottom of the page to help you if you struggle.

v	u	o	v	u	q	v
o	a	c	u	i	r	o
s	u	i	v	s	e	a
m	o	v	i	e	e	w
o	a	i	o	n	p	o
i	u	l	i	h	z	o
a	u	v	a	u	f	u

■ Write the words you have found on the lines.

■ Now write a sentence of your own for each word.

Clue: one vertical word, one horizontal word, two diagonal words.

Scholastic Literacy Skills
Handwriting: Years 5–6

PHOTOCOPIABLE
www.scholastic.co.uk

End-high horizontal joins

From 'arm' to 'worm'

■ Follow the instructions to change 'arm' to 'worm'.

> **consonants:** b c d f g h j k l m n p q r s t v w x y z
> **vowels:** a e i o u

arm

1. Add the fourth consonant to the beginning.

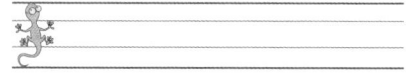

2. Change the vowel to the third vowel.

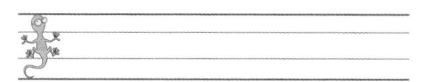

3. Change the initial letter to the 16th consonant and the vowel to the second vowel.

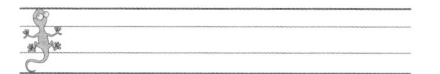

4. Change the initial letter to the 18th consonant and the vowel to the fourth vowel.

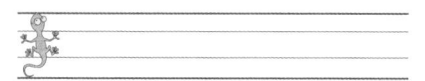

■ Try to make your own word chain by changing one letter at a time from 'harm' to 'warm'.

harm

warm

Chapter 1

End-high diagonal joins

Objective

To practise writing words with the end-high diagonal join using words with the letter strings 'ob', 'rh' and 'wl'.

Background knowledge

The end-high join to ascending letters 'b', 'h', 'k', 'l' and 't' needs careful teaching. Remind the children that the join takes them to where the next letter starts. In this case, the start of these is at the top of each letter. Encourage the children to use a slight curve, as going sharply up can slow writing and make the letters too close together.

Teach children to end high and curve up to the start of the letter. Remind them to finish the letter first before travelling from the end of the letter to the start of the next. This will avoid the letters sitting on top of each other.

Left-handers may wish to lift their pen from the paper while joining, thus avoiding having to push awkwardly across the page. If the ink or pencil trace disappears, do not tell them they have to produce a joining mark. However, do ensure they are joining just above the paper, rather than printing.

Activities

- **Photocopiable page 29 'Dictionary'**
The children write seven words that have the 'ob' letter string into a grid as a dictionary head word, practising using the end-high diagonal join. They then write their own definition for each word and check it with a dictionary. They are then asked to use each word in a sentence of their own to show how the word is used.

- **Photocopiable page 30 'Rhyming rhinos'**
In this activity, the children are given six words with the 'rh' letter string. They practise the end-high diagonal join by completing sentences, each with two gaps that require the same word. They then write three of the given words (rhino, rhyme and rhymes) that share the same vowel sound.

- **Photocopiable page 31 'Shapes'**
This activity focuses on words ending in the 'wl' letter string. First, children are challenged to see how many times they can write 'wl' inside a shape, while practising the end-high diagonal join. Then they write the opening paragraph to a story using a 'wl' word bank. This will help the children to practise joining to 'wl' using end-low diagonal and end-high horizontal joins.

Further ideas

- **Dictionary words:** Provide the children with dictionaries. Ask them to find as many words as they can containing the 'rh' letter string and to write them down inside a given time. Compare how many the children found and ask them to say if their handwriting remained neat in the timed activity. The activity can be repeated with the other letter strings that share the end-high diagonal join.
- **Word pictures:** Ask the children to draw an outline picture or shape to illustrate each of the words in this section and make a 'word picture' by filling in the outline with repetitions of the word it represents. They could also create a word picture by writing the word repeatedly to create the shape it represents.

What's on the CD-ROM

On the CD-ROM you will find:
- Animation of the joins.
- All of the photocopiable pages.

Scholastic Literacy Skills
Handwriting: Years 5–6

Name: Chapter 1

End-high diagonal joins

Dictionary

■ Create a dictionary. Write each word into the grid, add your own definition of the word and then check it with a dictionary.

■ Don't forget, words in a dictionary are written in alphabetical order.

job   sob   obey   robe   rob   robot   globe

Word	My definition	The dictionary definition

■ Now use each word in a sentence of your own that shows how it is used.

PHOTOCOPIABLE

Scholastic Literacy Skills
Handwriting: Years 5–6

Chapter 1   Name:

End-high diagonal joins

Rhyming rhinos

■ Which words are needed to make sense of these sentences?

| rhombus | perhaps | rhythm |
| rhyme | rhymes | rhino |

1. Sometimes lines of poetry _____ but some poems do not _____ at all.

2. A _____ is a large African animal with very thick skin and a large horn, but the _____ is now an endangered species.

3. Dancers need to hear the _____ of music and then they can use _____ in their dancing.

4. _____ it will rain but _____ it will be sunny.

5. Daisy _____ with crazy, and lolly _____ with dolly.

6. A _____ is a four-sided shape, but a square is not a _____ .

■ Which three words have the same vowel sound?
_____   _____   _____

Scholastic Literacy Skills
30 Handwriting: Years 5–6

PHOTOCOPIABLE

SCHOLASTIC
www.scholastic.co.uk

Name:

Chapter 1

End-high diagonal joins

Shapes

■ How many times can you write 'wl' into these shapes?

■ Write an opening paragraph to a story about a wolf. Use as many of the following words as you can.

| owl | bowl | sprawl | scowl | growl | prowl | howl | crawl |

PHOTOCOPIABLE

Scholastic Literacy Skills
Handwriting: Years 5–6   31

Chapter 1

End-high drop-on joins

Objective

To practise writing words with the end-high drop-on join using words with the letter strings 'oc', 'rd' and 'va'.

Background knowledge

The end-high join to drop-on letters needs explicit teaching. Here, the focus is on the letters 'a', 'd' and 'o'. Remind the children that the join takes them to where the next letter starts. In this case, the start of the drop-on letter is over at 1 o'clock, not 12 o'clock.

Teach children to end high, go straight across and drop on to the start of the letter. Going straight across will also avoid descending loopy joins that hinder legibility. Remind them to finish the letter first before travelling from the end of the letter to the start of the next. This will avoid the letters sitting on top of each other.

Left-handers may wish to lift their pen from the paper while joining, thus avoiding having to push awkwardly across the page. If the ink or pencil trace disappears, do not tell them they have to produce a joining mark. However, do ensure they are joining just above the paper, rather than printing.

Activities

● **Photocopiable page 33 'Rhymes'**
This photocopiable sheet provides four pictures of words ending in '-ock' to practise the end-high drop-on join (sock, rock, dock, block). The children then gain further practice by generating a list of more words that rhyme with '-ock', thus practising their knowledge of rhyming words while also practising the join.

● **Photocopiable page 34 'Same sound, different spelling'**
The children find four words in a wordsearch grid (herd, bird, ward and chord) and write them on the lines below, practising the end-high drop-on join. Ask the children to highlight, circle or underline the words in the grid before writing them. Encourage them to say the words aloud and listen to the vowel sound, before writing the words with the same vowel sound but different spelling on the lines below as pairs.

● **Photocopiable page 35 'Clues'**
In this activity, the children answer clues to find the correct word (van, vat, lava and oval) and practise writing the end-high drop-on join using the letter string 'va'. They then have further practice in the join by using the words in sentences of their own.

Further ideas

● **Eyes closed:** Ask the children to write one of the words from this section, then close their eyes and write it again underneath. Ask them to check if there are any differences in the handwriting between the two words. Ask them to write another word, close their eyes and try to write it again, but this time exactly on top of the first word.

● **Wiggly words:** Ask the children to practise writing the words along different-shaped lines such as zigzags and wiggly lines.

What's on the CD-ROM

On the CD-ROM you will find:
● Animation of the joins.
● All of the photocopiable pages.

End-high drop-on joins

Rhymes

■ Label these pictures with rhyming '-ock' words.

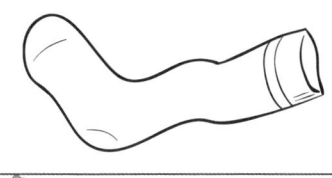

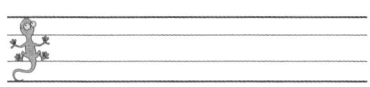

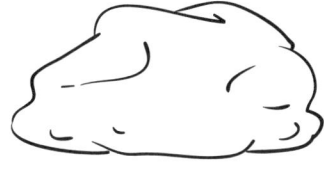

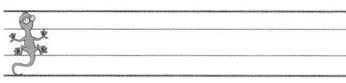

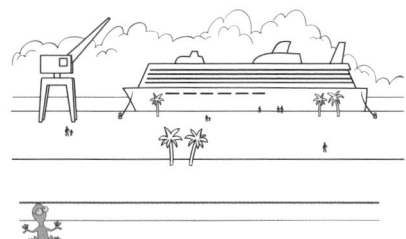

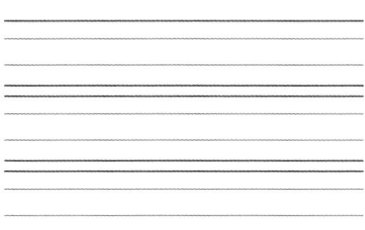

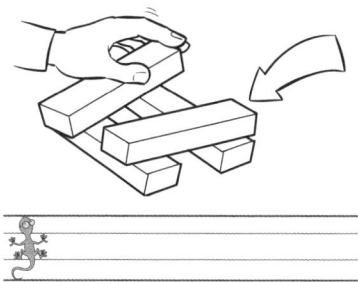

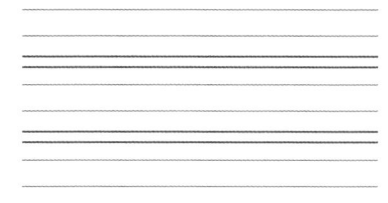

■ Now write the words in alphabetical order.

■ How many more rhyming words can you think of that end in '-ock'? Add them to the list.

■ Write a poem using the '-ock' words above.

Chapter 1　　　　　　　　　　Name:

End-high drop-on joins

Same sound, different spelling

■ Find the four words hidden in the wordsearch. Write them on the lines below.

o	a	w	g	h	w	a
f	x	c	h	o	r	d
m	n	d	e	p	q	s
g	b	i	r	d	r	b
w	a	r	d	o	f	w
a	s	f	h	i	k	l
e	d	b	r	r	d	e

■ Write a sentence of your own for each of the words.

_____
_____
_____
_____
_____
_____

■ Put the words that have the same vowel sound but different spellings together as a pair on the lines below.

_____   _____
_____   _____

Scholastic Literacy Skills
34　Handwriting: Years 5–6

PHOTOCOPIABLE

SCHOLASTIC
www.scholastic.co.uk

Clues

■ Answer the clues to match the words.

| oval   van   lava   vat |

1. Something used by workmen to transport their equipment by road.

2. Large tank or tub containing liquid.

3. This pours out of an active volcano.
   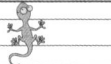

4. An elongated circle, also the name of the President's office in the United States.
   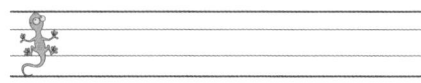

■ Use the words in sentences of your own.

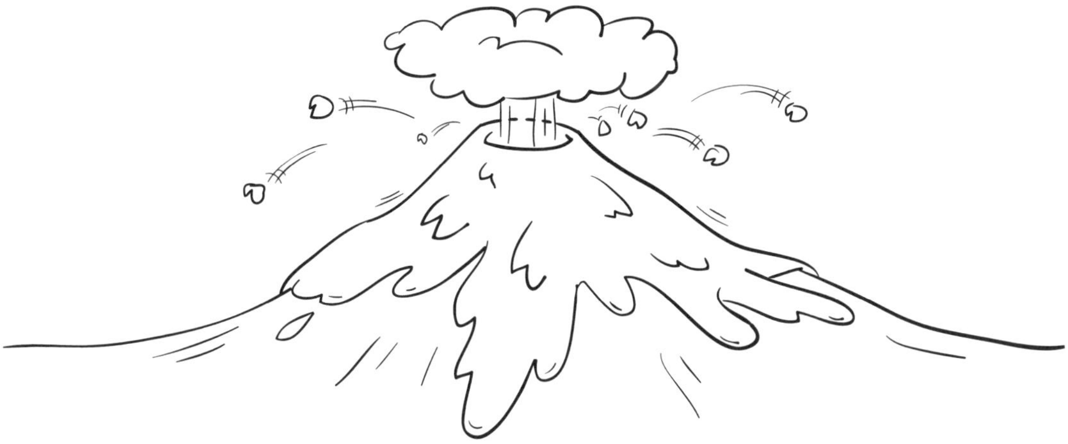

Chapter 1

End-high to 'e' joins

Objective

To practise writing words with the end-high to 'e' join using words with the letter strings 've', 're', and 'oe'.

Background knowledge

The end-high join to the letter 'e' needs explicit teaching separate from the other up, backwards and around shapes. If formed incorrectly, children will form their 'e' too high (above the top of the body line).

Remind children that the join takes them to where the next letter starts. In this case, the start of the drop-on letter is not over at 1 o'clock, but more in the middle of the clock.

Rather than teaching the children to end high and go straight across and drop on to the start of the letter, teach them to end high, curve slightly downwards and angle back up into the letter formation. It is important children do not go too far down to avoid forming an extra stroke.

Left-handers may wish to lift their pen from the paper while joining, thus avoiding having to push awkwardly across the page. If the ink or pencil trace disappears, do not tell them they have to produce a joining mark. However, do ensure they are joining just above the paper, rather than printing.

Activities

● **Photocopiable page 37 'Definitions'**
In this activity, the children expand six definitions of five words that have the 've' letter string, practising the end-high join to 'e'. They then have further practice by writing a sentence of their own for each word.

● **Photocopiable page 38 'School trip'**
The children fill in the gaps in a paragraph describing a school trip, choosing the missing words from a word bank (acre, agree, area, reach, threw). The focus for handwriting is the end-high join to 'e' using the 're' letter string. They practise further by arranging the list of words from the word bank into alphabetical order.

● **Photocopiable page 39 'Answers please'**
In this activity, the children are given an initial letter and a clue to eight different words (doe, foe, toe, poem, shoe, canoe, echoes, whoever) that all share the 'oe' letter string. They practise using the end-high to 'e' join when writing the answers. They then practise further by identifying the three rhyming words and one with a different pronunciation (whoever). You can make the activity more challenging by masking the word bank before doing the activity.

Further ideas

● **Recounts:** Encourage the children to write their own recounts of a school trip that they enjoyed.
● **Dictation:** The children could sit back to back, one describing a school trip orally while writing what they are describing. The other child writes what the first child is describing at the same time. Compare both recounts. Did the child who was taking dictation recreate the first child's recount accurately?
● **Dictionary:** Provide the children with dictionaries. Ask them to see how many words they can find containing the 'oe' letter string and write them down inside a given time. Repeat the activity with the words containing the 've' letter string.

What's on the CD-ROM

On the CD-ROM you will find:
● Animation of the joins.
● All of the photocopiable pages.

Scholastic Literacy Skills
Handwriting: Years 5–6

Name: Chapter 1

End-high to 'e' joins

Definitions

■ Read these words and their short definitions.

vet: type of doctor   **prove:** give evidence
cove: small bay   **wave:** flap your hand
cave: hole in a rock   **wave:** movement of water

■ Now write each word and a full definition. Check in a dictionary if you need help.

■ Use each word/meaning in a sentence of your own.

| vet | cove | cave | prove | wave | wave |

Chapter 1 Name:

End-high to 'e' joins

School trip

■ Choose words from the word bank to fill the gaps in the account of a school trip.

| area | threw | agree | acre | reach |

The School Trip

Our class went to the Country Farm last week. The children's ___(1)___ was quite small but there were some cute animals to see. The farmer said the field was about one ___(2)___ in size. Everyone had a good time, apart from Marcus who ___(3)___ his lunch into one of the pens. He tried to ___(4)___ it but it was eaten by a goat. He was in trouble! We wrote about the event today, and we all ___(5)___ that it was an enjoyable school trip.

1.
2.
3.
4.
5.

■ Now write the words into an alphabetical list, left to right.

Name: Chapter 1

End-high to 'e' joins

Answers please

■ Solve the clues to discover these 'oe' words.

| canoe | toe | poem | foe | whoever | doe | shoe | echoes |

A female deer. **Answer:** _____

An enemy. **Answer:** _____

There are five on each foot. **Answer:** _____

Made up of descriptive verses. **Answer:** _____

Worn on the feet outdoors. **Answer:** _____

A boat with pointed ends. **Answer:** _____

A sound that comes back to you. **Answer:** _____

Any person or people. **Answer:** _____

■ Which three words rhyme?

_____

■ Which word containing 'oe' is pronounced with the two separate phonemes /w/ and /e/?

_____

PHOTOCOPIABLE
www.scholastic.co.uk

Scholastic Literacy Skills
Handwriting: Years 5–6   39

Chapter 1

Tricky joins

Objective

To practise tricky joins 'ss', 'ff' and 'x'.

Background knowledge

Double 's' is covered in the tricky join section as a medial 's' changes shape. Double 'f' is a tricky movement in a small space and 'x' is a tricky join owing to the need to remove your pencil from the paper.

'ss' – As this letter form will only ever appear in the middle or at the end of a word, both 's's will be the alternative style. Teach children that they do not need to go over to the drop on. Instead, end low, curve up (like the curve in end-high diagonal joins) and stop when they hit the top of the body line, as if at 12 o'clock. Draw their pencil slightly back down the stroke they have just made before forming the bottom curl of the 's'. Ensure the children curl all the way back before continuing.

'ff' – Teach children this is a diagonal join from an end-low letter. Ensure the vertical stroke of the 'f' is straight and that they do not add a superfluous cross bar as the end-low join replaces this.

'x' – The letter 'x' is particularly tricky. To make the join the pen should be taken to the top left of the 'x' and then down towards the right. The pen is then taken off the page to complete the other part of the 'x' (top right to bottom left) before going back to the end of the first line to join from there to the next letter. Joining to, and from, 'x' uses different joins depending on the letter before and after. The letter 'o' joins to 'x' using the end-high horizontal join ('fox', 'box'), whereas 'a', 'e' and 'i' use the end-low diagonal join ('axe', 'exit', 'six'). The letter 'x' is a particularly tricky join and if children are struggling when trying to join it, then advise them not to join it.

Activities

- **Photocopiable page 41 'Guess with double 's''**
The children answer questions in a quiz. Each answer contains 'ss' (messy, guess, less, miss, floss, lesson). The children could discuss the questions and answers first with a partner before writing the answers. Encourage them to practise writing the join again by using the answers in new sentences.
- **Photocopiable page 42 'Double 'f' wordsearch'**
Hidden in the wordsearch are five words with 'ff' in them (raffle, effort, afford, coffee, sniff). Invite the children to find the words and write them in the spaces. To help the children, encourage them to circle or highlight the words in the wordsearch first.
- **Photocopiable page 43 'Max the pirate'**
In this activity, the children are given a treasure map. Illustrated on the map are five things that use the letter 'x' in their spellings. Ask the children to follow the route on the map and then write a description of the route from the cove to the exit, adding what they will see along the way. (Including: six (trees), x marks the spot, fox, axe and exit) Encourage them to add as much detail as they can.

Further ideas

- **Quiz:** Encourage the children to write their own quiz questions for words with the 'ss', 'ff' and 'x' spellings. Let them share their quiz with a partner or small group.

What's on the CD-ROM

On the CD-ROM you will find:
- Animation of the joins.
- All of the photocopiable pages.

Scholastic Literacy Skills
Handwriting: Years 5–6

Name: Chapter 1

Tricky joins

Guess with double 's'

■ All the answers to this quiz are words that end in 'ss'.

1. What is another word for 'untidy'?

2. What can you sometimes do when you don't know the answer?

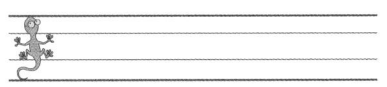

3. What is the opposite of 'more'?

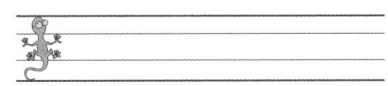

4. What is the title given to an unmarried woman?

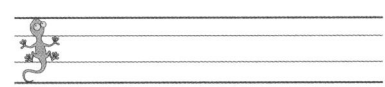

5. What do you use after brushing your teeth to clean in the gaps?

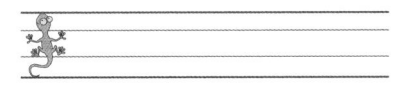

6. What is the name given to a time learning a subject at school?

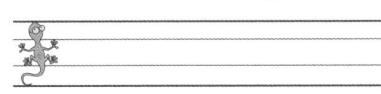

■ Now use each word in a new sentence. Practise joining the 'ss' letters neatly.

1.

2.

3.

4.

5.

6.

SCHOLASTIC   PHOTOCOPIABLE   Scholastic Literacy Skills
www.scholastic.co.uk   Handwriting: Years 5–6   41

Chapter 1   Name:

Tricky joins

Double 'f' wordsearch

■ Hidden in this wordsearch are five words with double 'f'.
■ Find the words and write them in the space below. To help you, first draw a ring round or highlight each word.

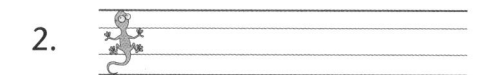

t	r	e	e	q	f	c	h
r	a	f	f	l	e	o	o
a	f	f	o	r	d	f	f
p	y	o	f	c	a	f	e
s	l	r	d	e	b	e	n
f	e	t	z	x	r	e	d
c	a	n	s	n	i	f	f

1. _____   2. _____

3. _____   4. _____

5. _____

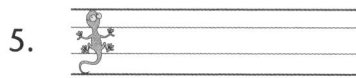

■ Now use each word in a sentence to show its meaning.

_____
_____
_____
_____
_____
_____
_____
_____
_____
_____

Scholastic Literacy Skills
Handwriting: Years 5–6

PHOTOCOPIABLE

SCHOLASTIC
www.scholastic.co.uk

Name: Chapter 1

Tricky joins

Max the pirate

■ Max the pirate has hidden his treasure on an island. He orders his crew to sail to the island and bring back the treasure. To help his crew, he has drawn a map.

■ Your task is to describe the route that Max took, adding what he met and saw along the way. Ensure you use at least five words with 'x' in them.

Chapter 2

Suffixes

Introduction

This chapter focuses on practising handwriting using different joins to add suffixes to words. It includes looking at words ending in 'e' and 'y', adding suffixes that begin with a vowel, transforming verbs into nouns and nouns into verbs, using comparatives and adding other suffixes '-ology', '-ance' and '-ise'.

When the children are practising handwriting, they are also practising spelling, focusing on adding suffixes to root words. When adding a vowel suffix to some root words, the spelling of the root word alters, for example, if the root word ends in 'e', the final 'e' of the route is dropped; if the root word ends in y, the y is dropped. When adding a consonant suffix to most root words, the spelling rule is simply to add the suffix without altering the root.

The activities in this chapter allow practice of a variety of joins while focusing on specific spellings. All children will benefit from rewriting these letter strings repeatedly, so you may wish to encourage them to do some extra practice either on paper or individual whiteboards. Where children are experiencing difficulty with particular spelling patterns, give them time for extra handwriting practice on the part of the words that are giving them the problem, in order to educate the hand into the right movements when joining the problem letters – it is rare for a child to get every letter in a word wrong. Once the letter string has been practised, the child should then write whole words containing that spelling pattern, for further reinforcement.

In this chapter

Adding a suffix page 45	To practise adding suffixes to words ending in 'e' and 'y'.
Transforming nouns to verbs page 49	To change nouns into verbs by adding the suffixes '-ate', '-en' and '-ify'.
Transforming verbs to nouns page 53	To change verbs to nouns using the suffixes '-ity', '-ism' and '-ness'.
Comparatives page 57	To practise forming comparatives using '-er', '-est' and '-like'.
Other suffixes page 61	To practise using the suffixes '-ology', '-ance' and '-ise' to root words to form nouns and verbs.

Adding a suffix

Objective

To practise adding suffixes to words ending in 'e' and 'y'.

Background knowledge

Adding a suffix to a word modifies its meaning and changes its word class. Sometimes the spelling of the root word needs to be altered when adding a suffix, particularly for words ending in a vowel or 'y' when adding a suffix that begins with a vowel.

When joining to 'e', remind the children that the join takes them to where the next letter starts. In this case, the start of the drop-on letter is not over at 1 o'clock, but more in the middle of the clock.

Descender letters should be treated in exactly the same way. When forming the join, remind children to finish the letter first before travelling from the end of the letter to the start of the next. This will avoid the letters sitting on top of each other.

Left-handers may wish to lift their pen from the paper while joining, thus avoiding having to push awkwardly across the page. If the ink or pencil trace disappears, do not tell them they have to produce a joining mark. However, do ensure they are joining just above the paper, rather than printing. Left-handers may also want to produce a sharper, more italic-style exit to their end-low joins. This is fine as long as they leave enough space between their words and don't cramp their letters together.

Activities

- **Photocopiable page 46 "-ing', '-est' or '-ish'?'**
This activity focuses on three common suffixes: '-ing', '-est' and '-ish'. The children must choose which suffix to use and practise the spelling rule of dropping the final 'e' when adding a suffix that begins with a vowel. These suffixes use a combination of joins, including end-low diagonal and end-low drop-on. There is also one end-high join to 'e' – in 'rarest' – that the children need to take care in forming.

- **Photocopiable page 47 'Suffixes (1)'**
In this activity, the suffixes '-ment', '-ness', '-ful' and '-less' are added to words ending in 'e'. These suffixes use a range of joins and the children should be particularly careful about 'ss' and remember that both 's's will be the second style. The end-low diagonal join from 'e' is used in every word. The children choose which suffix(es) to add to each word and write a sentence using the new word.

- **Photocopiable page 48 'Suffixes (2)'**
Suffixes from the previous two activities are covered again here, this time used when adding them to a root word ending in 'y'. The children will practise a variety of joins to/from 'i' as they change the 'y' to an 'i' to add the suffix. They must choose a suffix to make a new word and use it in a sentence. Some of the root words can use more than one suffix, so writing a sentence ensures they understand the meaning of the new word and practises their handwriting at the same time.

Further ideas

- **Root + suffix snap:** Provide pairs of children with suffix and root cards. Ask the pairs to play a variation of 'Snap'. One child places a root card down and the other places a suffix card. When they find two cards that make a plausible combination, they must write the word down using their best handwriting.

What's on the CD-ROM

On the CD-ROM you will find:
- Animation of the joins.
- All of the photocopiable pages.

Chapter 2   Name:

Adding a suffix

'-ing', '-est' or '-ish'?

■ Change the word in bold to make sense of each sentence by adding '-ing', '-est' or '-ish'.
■ Remember to drop the final 'e' when adding a suffix that starts with a vowel, for example **hate – hating**, **fine – finest**, **square – squarish**.
■ Rewrite the word in bold with the correct suffix below the sentence.

1. After the game, everyone was **smile**.

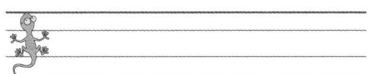

2. This is the **nice** present I have ever had!

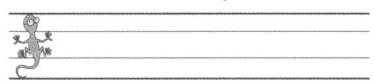

3. This new shirt is really **style**!

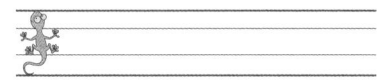

4. Isn't that the **cute** kitten of them all?

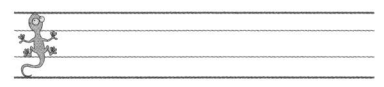

5. First sun then rain; I wish the weather would stop **change**.

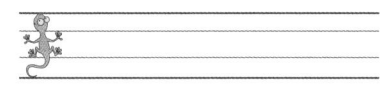

6. Out of all these animals, the tiger is the **rare**.

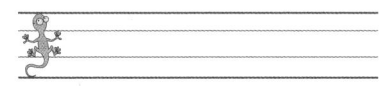

7. He was **hope** to get full marks for the maths test.

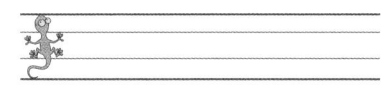

8. The paint is not really a pure blue, but it is **blue**.

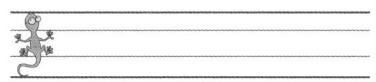

9. John is close, Kim is closer, but Kashif is **close**.

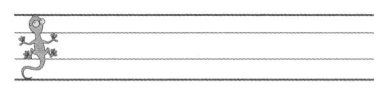

10. I am **ride** my bike to school today.

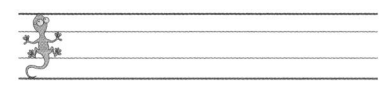

Scholastic Literacy Skills
46 Handwriting: Years 5–6

PHOTOCOPIABLE

www.scholastic.co.uk

Name: Chapter 2

Adding a suffix

Suffixes (1)

■ When you add a suffix that starts with a consonant, such as '-ment', '-ness', '-ful' and '-less', to a word that ends in 'e', there is no need to drop the 'e'.

■ Draw a line to match each word with the correct suffix, then write the words with their suffixes on the lines. Some of the words can have two of the suffixes.

| care |
| announce |
| entice |
| grace |
| manage |
| use |

| ment |
| ful |
| less |

■ Now write some sentences using some of the new words.

SCHOLASTIC   PHOTOCOPIABLE   Scholastic Literacy Skills
www.scholastic.co.uk   Handwriting: Years 5–6   47

Chapter 2

Adding a suffix

Suffixes (2)

- Take care when adding a suffix to words ending in 'y'. Drop the 'y' and add 'i'.
- Choose one suffix from the box to add to each word below.

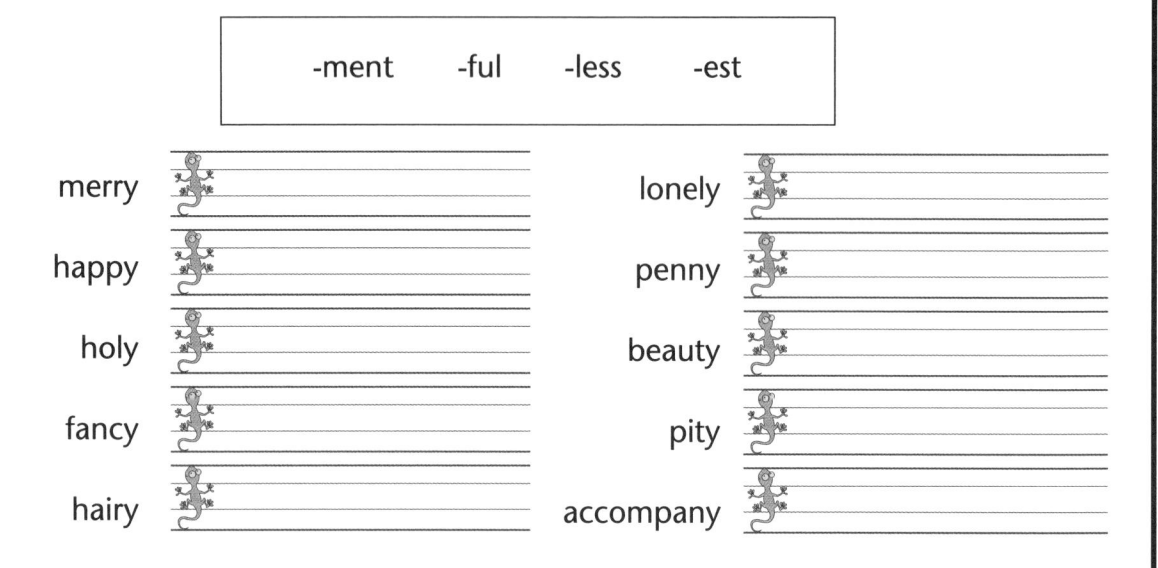

| -ment | -ful | -less | -est |

merry

happy

holy

fancy

hairy

lonely

penny

beauty

pity

accompany

- Write five sentences to use the new words.

Scholastic Literacy Skills
Handwriting: Years 5–6

PHOTOCOPIABLE
www.scholastic.co.uk

Chapter 2

Transforming nouns to verbs

Objective

To change nouns into verbs by adding the suffixes '-ate', '-en' and '-ify'.

Background knowledge

Adding a suffix to a word modifies its meaning and changes the word class. Sometimes the root word also alters when a suffix is added.

For the end-high drop-on join from 'r' or 'o' to 'c' and 'a', remind children that the join takes them to where the next letter starts. In this case, the start of the drop-on letter is over at 1 o'clock, not 12 o'clock. This formation avoids gaps in the top of the letter.

For joining 'r' to 'e', rather than teaching the children to end high and go straight across and drop on to the start of the letter, teach them to end high, curve slightly downwards and angle back up into the letter formation. It is important children do not go too far down; they should avoid forming an extra stroke.

Activities

- **Photocopiable page 50 'Nouns to verbs (1)'**
The focus suffix in this activity is '-ate'. Each new verb allows the children to practise using the end-low drop-on join to the letter 'a' from the letters 'n', 't' and 'l', and the end-high drop-on join to 'a' from the letter 'r'. The children practise writing and spelling nouns that can be changed into verbs by adding the suffix '-ate'. Remind them that, when adding a suffix that begins with the vowel 'a' to a root word that ends with a vowel, the final vowel of the root is dropped.

- **Photocopiable page 51 'Nouns to verbs (2)'**
In this activity the children change six nouns to verbs by adding the suffix '-en'. Writing each new verb enables the children to practise all the joins and specifically the end-low drop-on join to the letter 'e' – remind the children to go through the middle of the clock and that it is the second style. The last two nouns alter the root word when changing them to verbs, so ask the children to take extra care here. You could ask them to check their answers with a dictionary.

- **Photocopiable page 52 'Changing nouns to verbs ending in '-ify"**
The children practise writing verbs that end in the suffix '-ify'. Remind them that for the drop-on join to 'f' they need to go over to 1 o'clock before starting to form their letter. The nouns end in both consonants and vowels; this will reinforce the spelling rule to drop the final vowel of a noun when adding a suffix that starts with a vowel, and simply to add the suffix to nouns that end in consonants. Two of the nouns ('terror' and 'horror') do not conform to either pattern so the children can practise their handwriting by inventing a rule to apply to these two words. (The adjectives are: solid, pure, simple, class, horror.)

Further ideas

- **Suffix count:** Working in pairs, one child calls out as many words as they can that use the suffixes in a limited time, while their partner writes them down. Allow them to use the words from the activities in this section as well as any new ones they can think of. Tell the one calling out the words they must wait while one word is fully written before calling out another. Then swap over.

What's on the CD-ROM

On the CD-ROM you will find:
- Animation of the joins.
- All of the photocopiable pages.

Chapter 2

Transforming nouns to verbs

Nouns to verbs (1)

■ Use a dictionary to find the meaning of these nouns. Write the definition in the first space.

■ Then make a verb by adding '-ate' to the noun and write it in the second space.

■ Check your spelling with a dictionary.

Noun	Definition	Verb
pollen		
decor		
hyphen		
orchestra		
rota		
formula		
assassin		

■ Now write a sentence using each new verb.

Scholastic Literacy Skills
Handwriting: Years 5–6

Transforming nouns to verbs

Nouns to verbs (2)

■ The nouns below can be changed into verbs by adding the suffix '-en', for example **length** – **lengthen**.

1. If you increase something's **strength**, you do what to it?

2. If you give some people a **fright**, you do what to them?

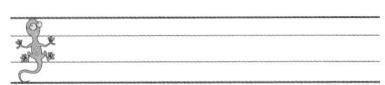

3. If you make a **threat** to someone, you do what to him?

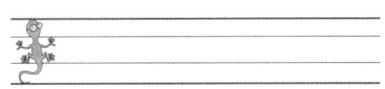

4. If you make something **damp**, you do what to it?

■ Now change these two nouns into verbs.

width   depth

■ Now write your own sentences using the verbs.

Chapter 2   Name:

Transforming nouns to verbs

Changing nouns to verbs ending in '-ify'

- Change these nous into verbs.

Take care:
- When adding a suffix that starts with a vowel to a word that ends with a vowel.
- When adding a suffix that starts with a vowel to a word that ends in 'y'.
- When adding a suffix to 'terror' and 'horror'.

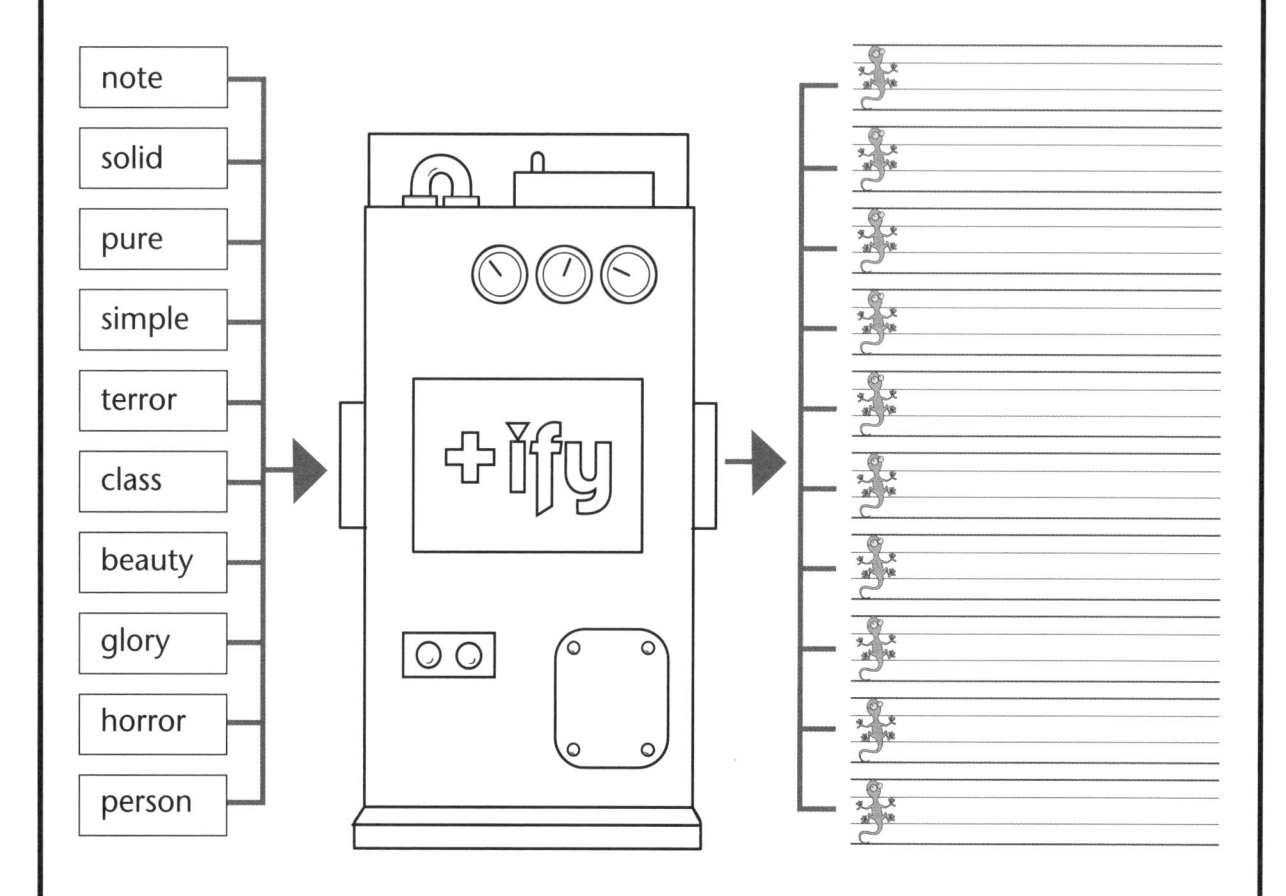

note
solid
pure
simple
terror
class
beauty
glory
horror
person

+ify

- **Word classes:** Can you find the words in the list that are adjectives?
_____
_____

- Write a spelling rule that applies to 'terror' and 'horror'.
_____
_____
_____
_____

Scholastic Literacy Skills
Handwriting: Years 5–6

PHOTOCOPIABLE
SCHOLASTIC
www.scholastic.co.uk

Transforming verbs to nouns

Objective

To change verbs to nouns using the suffixes '-ity', '-ism' and '-ness'.

Background knowledge

Certain verbs can be changed into nouns by adding a suffix. When the root word ends in the vowel 'e' and the suffix begins with a vowel, as in '-ity' and '-ism', the final vowel of the root word is dropped. When the suffix begins with a consonant, as in '-ness', it is simply added to the root word, whatever the final letter.

To join root words to these suffixes, different joins will be used depending on the final letter of the root and the beginning letter of the suffix, including the end-low diagonal and the end-high horizontal join.

Left-handers may wish to lift their pen from the paper while joining, thus avoiding having to push awkwardly across the page. If the ink or pencil trace disappears, do not tell them they have to produce a joining mark. However, do ensure they are joining just above the paper, rather than printing. Left-handers may also want to produce a sharper, more italic-style exit to their end-low joins. This is fine as long as they leave enough space between their words and don't cramp their letters together.

Activities

- **Photocopiable page 54 'Verbs to nouns (1)'**
The children change a verb in a sentence into a noun by adding the suffix '-ity'. They practise the end-low diagonal join from the letters 'u', 't', 'd', 'l' and 's' to 'i', and the end-high horizontal join from 'r' and 'v' to 'i'. Certain root words need care as the root changes when a suffix is added ('brief' to 'brevity').

- **Photocopiable page 55 'Verbs to nouns (2)'**
In this activity, the children are given five verbs ending in '-ise' and asked to change them to nouns by adding the suffix '-ism'. Remind them that the second form of 's' will be used in the suffix. They practise a number of different types of join including end-high horizontal and diagonal joins. Remind the children about dropping the final 'e' of the root word before adding a vowel suffix.

- **Photocopiable page 56 'Verbs and adjectives to nouns using '-ness"**
The children are given a list of verbs and adjectives to change into nouns by adding the suffix '-ness'. The joins they practise are the end-low diagonal join, and the end-high horizontal and drop-on joins. When adding this consonant suffix, the children do not need to alter the root word when they add the suffix, unless the root word ends in 'y'. They have further practice by choosing three of the nouns to use in sentences, thus demonstrating an understanding of the meaning and use of the nouns.

Further ideas

- **Alliterative sentences:** Ask the children to choose words from the activities in this section and write alliterative sentences. Encourage them to have fun with the sentences; they can be silly sentences and don't need to make sense.

What's on the CD-ROM

On the CD-ROM you will find:
- Animation of the joins.
- All of the photocopiable pages.

Chapter 2　　　　　　　　　Name:

Transforming verbs to nouns

Verbs to nouns (1)

■ Some verbs can be changed into nouns by adding the suffix '-ity'.
■ Change the bold verbs into nouns. Be careful! Some of the root words' spellings change.

1. Please will you **clear** up the mess when you have finished?

2. I will **continue** the story after lunchtime.

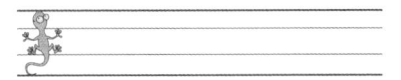

3. Let that cheese **mature** before you eat it.

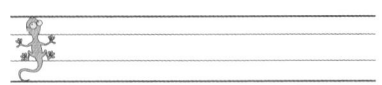

4. We should **unite** and work together.

■ Complete the sentences with a word that ends in '-ity'.

1. *When you are stupid you show* .
2. *When something is brief, it has* .
3. *A boy who is agile shows his* .
4. *When something is dense, it has* .

■ Place the new words into the table below.

Root word spelling changed	Remove 'e' and add suffix	Just add the suffix

Scholastic Literacy Skills
54　Handwriting: Years 5–6

Verbs to nouns (2)

- Some verbs can be changed into nouns by adding the suffix '-ism'.
- Put these verbs through the suffix machine to change them into the noun form.

Verb: criticise, baptise, terrorise, symbolise, plagiarise

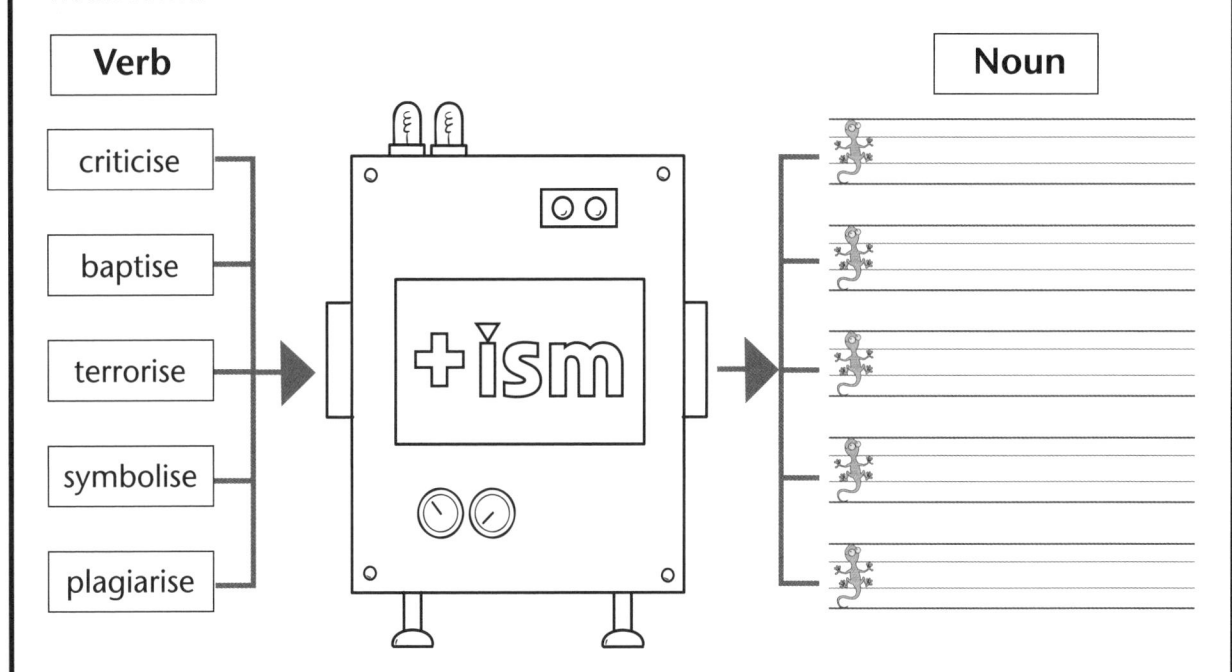

Noun: _____

- Write the correct noun to complete the sentence.

1. No matter how hard I try, I always get lots of _____.
2. Copying someone else's work is _____.
3. The baby's _____ will take place at St Mary's Church.
4. Acts of _____ can hurt innocent people.
5. Many religious buildings contain artwork that is full of _____.

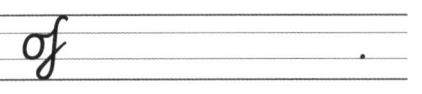

Chapter 2　　　　　　　　Name:

Transforming verbs to nouns

Verbs and adjectives to nouns using '-ness'

- Some verbs can be used as nouns when you add the suffix '-ness'.
- Change these verb phrases and adjectives into nouns by adding '-ness'.

Verb	Suffix		Noun
to forgive	+ ness	=	
to be ripe	+ ness	=	
to be numb	+ ness	=	
to look like	+ ness	=	
to be separate	+ ness	=	

Adjective	Suffix		Noun
happy	+ ness	=	
furry	+ ness	=	
dainty	+ ness	=	

- Choose three of the nouns from the list and use them in sentences.

Comparatives

Objective

To practise forming comparatives using '-er', '-est' and '-like'.

Background knowledge

Comparatives and superlatives are formed by adding the suffix '-er' and '-est' to adjectives. A comparison may also be made by adding the suffix '-like' to nouns.

When joining to 'e', remind the children that the join takes them to where the next letter starts. In this case, the start of the drop-on letter is not over at 1 o'clock, but more in the middle of the clock.

When joining descender letters, remind the children to go straight from the end of the letter to the start of the next.

Left-handers may wish to lift their pen from the paper while joining, thus avoiding having to push awkwardly across the page. If the ink or pencil trace disappears, do not tell them they have to produce a joining mark. However, do ensure they are joining just above the paper, rather than printing. Left-handers may also want to produce a sharper, more italic-style exit to their end-low joins. This is fine as long as they leave enough space between their words and don't cramp their letters together.

Activities

● **Photocopiable page 58 'Faster, higher, further'**
The children form comparatives by adding the suffix '-er' to adjectives in a sports context. The 'er' suffix uses an end-low diagonal join, but a range of joins will be covered when writing sentences. Remind children that they may need to use the second style of 'e' depending on the preceding letter. Most of the adjectives are formed by simply adding the suffix without changing the root word, apart from doubling the consonant for 'big' and changing the root for 'far'. Some children may need reminding or supporting when meeting those words.

● **Photocopiable page 59 'The most'**
In this activity, the children are given a list of adjectives and asked to form superlatives by adding the suffix '-est'. Remind the children that formation of 'e' might change depending on its preceding letter, and the 's' will be the second style. You might like to point out the words where the root word is changed when adding a vowel suffix (naughty, tasty), and also the words that end with a vowel (nice and late).

● **Photocopiable page 60 'Like a child'**
Here the children form comparisons by adding the suffix '-like' to the noun about which the comparison is being made. The children practise the end-low diagonal join to each of the letters in this suffix. Make sure the children avoid placing the loop of the 'k' too high, to resemble a capital 'R', or too low, to look like the letter 'b'.

Further ideas

● **Advert:** Encourage the children to write an advertisement for children to join the school athletics club, including what sorts of skills are required and why children would benefit from joining the club.
● **Tastiest meal:** Encourage the children to write a review in the style of a newspaper article of a recent meal they have eaten. They must use comparatives and superlatives.

What's on the CD-ROM

On the CD-ROM you will find:
● Animation of the joins.
● All of the photocopiable pages.

Chapter 2

Comparatives

Faster, higher, further

■ Sporty Sam always wants to improve! Copy the sentences and help him explain himself by using the root word in bold and changing it to make sense.

1. That jump is too low. Please make it **high**.

2. My time in that race was too slow. Let me do it again so I can go **fast**.

3. I am sure I can throw the javelin much **far** than that!

4. My bike is too small for me. I need a **big** one for racing.

5. I need a new tennis racket so I can hit the ball **hard**.

6. I am **strong** than the others, so I should be good at weightlifting.

Comparatives

The most

- When we compare more than two things, we use a superlative adjective by adding the suffix '-est', **longest day** for example.
- Add a superlative adjective to each of these nouns, and then use them in sentences.
- Take care with the spelling of tricky words.

Adjectives

| fast | naughty | bright | late | hard | nice | dark | high | tasty |

Nouns

| boy | cake | girl | light | colour | tower | fashion | time | sum |

Chapter 2 Name:

Comparatives

Like a child

■ Comparisons can be made with other things by adding the suffix '-like' to the noun that something is being compared with.

■ First, write these words into the table according to their word class.

child   alive   lady   dream   bird   marsh   dancing

Noun	Adjective	Verb

■ Now change the adjectives and verbs into nouns.

■ Write the comparative noun (using '-like') for the phrases in bold in these sentences.

1. Her behaviour is **like a child**.

2. The drawing looks **like it is alive**.

3. Her voice is not at all **like a lady**.

4. The play was **like a dream**.

5. Her appetite was **like a bird's**.

6. The muddy lawn is **like a marsh**.

7. The movement was quite **like dancing**.

Chapter 2

Other suffixes

Objective

To practise using the suffixes '-ology', '-ance' and '-ise' to root words to form nouns and verbs.

Background knowledge

For the drop-on joins to letters 'a' in '-ance' and 'o' in '-ology', remind the children that the join takes them to where the next letter starts. In this case, the start of the drop-on letter is over at 1 o'clock, not 12 o'clock. This formation avoids gaps in the top of the letter.

End low – Teach the children to end low, go up, go over and drop on to the start of the next letter.

End high – Teach the children to end high, go straight across and drop on to the start of the next letter. Going straight across will also avoid loopy joins that hinder legibility.

Descender letters should be treated in exactly the same way. When forming the join, remind children to finish the letter first before travelling from the end of the letter to the start of the next. This will avoid the letters sitting on top of each other.

Left-handers may wish to lift their pen from the paper while joining, thus avoiding having to push awkwardly across the page. If the ink or pencil trace disappears, do not tell them they have to produce a joining mark. However, do ensure they are joining just above the paper, rather than printing. Left-handers may also want to produce a sharper, more italic-style exit to their end-low joins. This is fine as long as they leave enough space between their words and don't cramp their letters together.

Activities

● **Photocopiable page 62 'Ologies'**
The first suffix featured in this section, '-ology', originates from the Greek 'logos' meaning 'study of'. Most words ending in '-ology' also use a word of Greek or Latin origin for the root word. An understanding of the Greek and Latin origins will help children's spelling and ability to work out meanings. The suffix '-ology' uses a combination of joins, including end-high diagonal, end-low drop-on, end-high drop-on and end-low diagonal. This wide variety of joins can make it a tricky letter string to form.

● **Photocopiable page 63 'Verbs to nouns (3)'**
The children change ten verbs into nouns by adding the suffix '-ance'. They will practise both the end-low and end-high drop-on joins to 'a' from 'r'. They then group the words according to whether they need to alter the root word before adding the suffix.

● **Photocopiable page 64 'Nouns to verbs (3)'**
The children use the suffix '-ise' to make adjectives (and nouns) into verbs. The children practise the end-high horizontal join and the end-low diagonal join to the letter 'i'. They need to write the definition of the adjective and then write the verb form. They can use a dictionary if they wish. Point out the tricky words to help them (harmony, deputy).

Further ideas

● **My ologies:** Ask the children to invent other words that could use the suffix '-ology', to mean the study of something, and write them in a list. See how many they can make up.

What's on the CD-ROM

On the CD-ROM you will find:
● Animation of the joins.
● All of the photocopiable pages.

Scholastic Literacy Skills
Handwriting: Years 5–6

Chapter 2　　　　　　　　　　Name:

Other suffixes

Ologies

- The suffix '-ology' means 'study of'.
- Use these root words with the suffix '-ology' to create words with the following meanings.

Root word	Meaning
bios	life
geo	earth
zoo	animal
chronos	time
ideo	ideas
psyche	mind
techno	craft, method

1. The study of life.

2. The study of animal life.

3. The study of the mind.

4. The study of how things are made.

5. The study of ideas.

6. The study of time.

7. The study of the Earth.

Scholastic Literacy Skills
Handwriting: Years 5–6

PHOTOCOPIABLE

www.scholastic.co.uk

Name: Chapter 2

Other suffixes

Verbs to nouns (3)

- Adding the suffix '-ance' to a verb changes it into a noun.
- Sometimes the root word needs changing before adding '-ance'.
- Change these verbs into nouns.

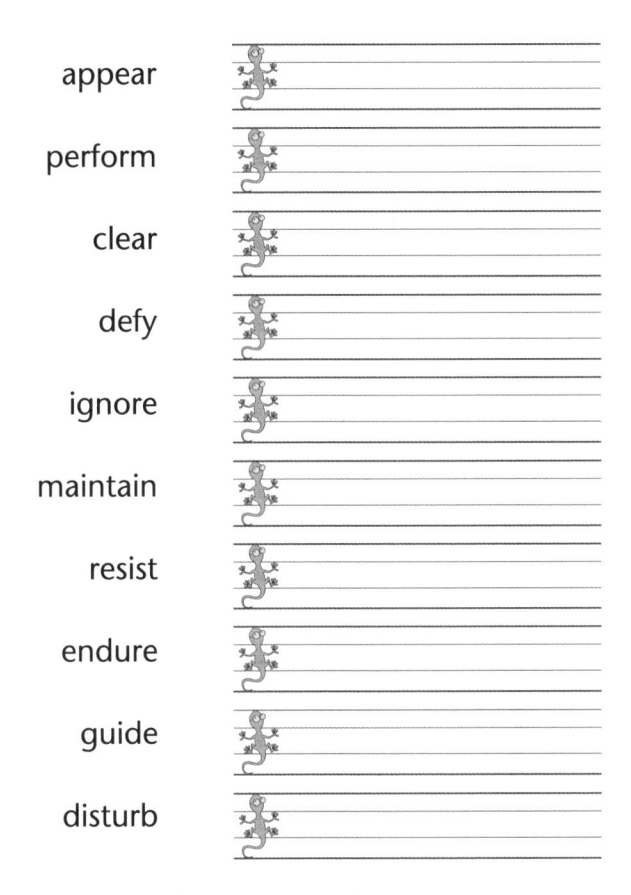

appear

perform

clear

defy

ignore

maintain

resist

endure

guide

disturb

- Now write the verbs in the correct column.

Root word stays the same	Root word needs to be changed

PHOTOCOPIABLE

Chapter 2

Name:

Other suffixes

Nouns to verbs (3)

- You can change some nouns and adjectives into verbs by adding the suffix '-ise'.
- Use a dictionary to find the meaning of each adjective and add it to the column.
- Change these adjectives into verbs by adding '-ise'.

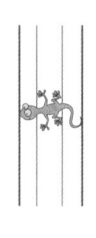

Noun	Adjective	Adjective meaning	Verb
family	familiar		
harmony	harmonious		
magnet	magnetic		
deputy	deputy		
final	final		
minimum	minimum		
maximum	maximum		
reality	real		
public	public		

Scholastic Literacy Skills
Handwriting: Years 5–6

PHOTOCOPIABLE

www.scholastic.co.uk

Chapter 3
Prefixes and word roots

Introduction

This chapter focuses on practising joining prefixes and common word roots. The activities begin with a revision section for prefixes encountered previously, 'un-', 'mis-' and 'dis-', using the end-low diagonal join, followed by sections on prefixes for negation and words with Latin roots.

Throughout the activities, the children's understanding of the meanings and usage of prefixes is reaffirmed through practice. The children write sentences to show their understanding and refer to dictionaries while writing definitions of their own. Handwriting is practised using a variety of joins, and particularly the most common forms: the end-low diagonal join and the end-high horizontal join.

The end-low diagonal join is the most common form of join. Children find the simplest joins to acquire are from letters that end at the writing line ('a', 'b', 'c', 'd', 'e', 'h', 'i', 'k', 'l', 'm', 'n', 's', 't', 'u', 'x' and 'z'). Some descender (tail) letters ('g', 'j', 'p', 'q' and 'y') are included in this too.

When dealing with drop-on joins, remind the children to go over to 1 o'clock to start their letters.

In this chapter

Prefix revision page 66	To practise using the prefixes 'un-', 'mis-' and dis-'.
Prefixes for negation (1) page 70	To practise writing words with the prefixes for negation 'il-', 'ir-' and 'in-'.
Prefixes for negation (2) page 74	To practise writing words with the prefixes for negation, 'im-', 'non-' and 'anti-'.
Words with a Latin root (1) page 78	To practise writing words using prefixes and word roots with Latin roots, 'prim-', 'aqua-' and 'multi-'.
Words with a Latin root (2) page 82	To practise writing words using prefixes and word roots with Latin roots, 'quad-', 'auto-' and 'mari-'.

Chapter 3

Prefix revision

Objective

To practise using the prefixes 'un-', 'mis-' and dis-'.

Background knowledge

When the prefixes 'un-', 'mis-' and 'dis-' are added to a root word they create a new word with an opposite or negative meaning. List words using these prefixes on the whiteboard and invite the children to take off the prefix and tell you what the root word means. Remind the children that not all words can have such prefixes added to make the opposite meaning. These activities could also lead to work on antonyms and synonyms.

Left-handers may wish to lift their pen from the paper while joining, thus avoiding having to push awkwardly across the page. If the ink or pencil trace disappears, do not tell them they have to produce a joining mark. However, do ensure they are joining just above the paper, rather than printing. Left-handers may also want to produce a sharper, more italic-style exit to their end-low joins. This is fine as long as they leave enough space between their words and don't cramp their letters together.

Activities

● **Photocopiable page 67 'Opposites'**
This activity gives the opportunity to revise and practise the full range of joins, particularly the end-low diagonal join in the prefix 'un-'. The children need to read the sentences and decide which word in each one can have the 'un-' prefix added to change the meaning. They write the amended sentence, and then create their own sentence using the new word in context while practising joining from 'un-' to a root word. Remind the children to form 'been' with two second style 'e's.

● **Photocopiable page 68 "dis' wordsearch'**
The focus here is the 'dis-' prefix, which consists of end-low diagonal and end-low drop-on joins. In this activity, children find eight words hidden in a wordsearch and write them underneath. (The words are: dissatisfy, disallow, displease, distrust, disuse, disappear, dissimilar, disagree.) They then have further practice in using the words in context by writing a new sentence for each word. They also practise the tricky 'ss' join for two of the words, 'dissimilar' and 'dissatisfy'. Warn the children to watch out for red herrings of the 'dis' letter string.

● **Photocopiable page 69 'Mistaken pairs'**
In this activity, children must choose the correct use of the prefix 'mis-' from seven paired words using the 'mis-', 'dis-' and 'un-' prefixes. They then write a sentence to show the use of each word in context while practising the end-low diagonal join. Make sure that the children are using the second style of 's' when it is preceded by another letter.

Further ideas

● **Reading examples:** From reading, collect other examples of negative prefixes, such as 'dis-', 'mal-' and 'de-', and practise joining them to root words.
● **Negative issues:** Find an issue in which the children are interested and ask them to write a letter that makes use of words with negative prefixes to get their point across. You could give them several appropriate words to start them off, such as 'unnecessary', 'misplaced', 'illegal', 'irresponsible' and so on.

What's on the CD-ROM

On the CD-ROM you will find:
● Animation of the joins.
● All of the photocopiable pages.

Name: Chapter 3

Prefix revision

Opposites

■ Change each sentence to the opposite meaning by adding the prefix 'un-' to one of the words.
■ Write the altered sentence.
■ Then write a sentence of your own using the same prefix word.

1. The family had a very pleasant walk up the hill.

2. Their behaviour has been acceptable today.

3. We are willing to join you on your long journey.

4. I thought the result of the match was surprising.

5. All the rooms on this corridor are occupied.

6. It is quite reasonable to expect everyone's homework will finished on time.

PHOTOCOPIABLE

Scholastic Literacy Skills
Handwriting: Years 5–6 67

Chapter 3 Name:

Prefix revision

'dis' wordsearch

■ Hidden in the grid are eight words that all start with the prefix 'dis-'. Highlight or circle the words.

■ Tip: Watch out for double 's' consonants.

m	d	i	s	s	a	t	i	s	f	y
i	l	d	i	s	a	l	l	o	w	d
s	d	i	p	e	n	d	i	s	a	i
d	i	s	p	l	e	a	s	e	d	s
i	s	s	o	h	b	g	o	t	i	u
s	a	i	d	i	s	t	r	u	s	t
l	p	m	a	d	i	s	h	e	a	j
k	p	i	c	d	k	g	r	a	g	r
e	e	l	d	i	s	u	s	e	r	s
p	a	a	e	s	n	o	k	n	e	p
x	r	r	j	e	p	o	p	l	e	n

■ Write the words you have found here.

■ Now write a sentence for each word.

Prefix revision

Mistaken pairs

- Which word in each of these pairs uses the right prefix?
- Circle each correct one, then use it in a sentence of your own.

misbehave	disbehave
unjudge	misjudge
discalculate	miscalculate
unplaced	misplaced
mislead	dislead
mistreat	distreat
misunderstood	disunderstood

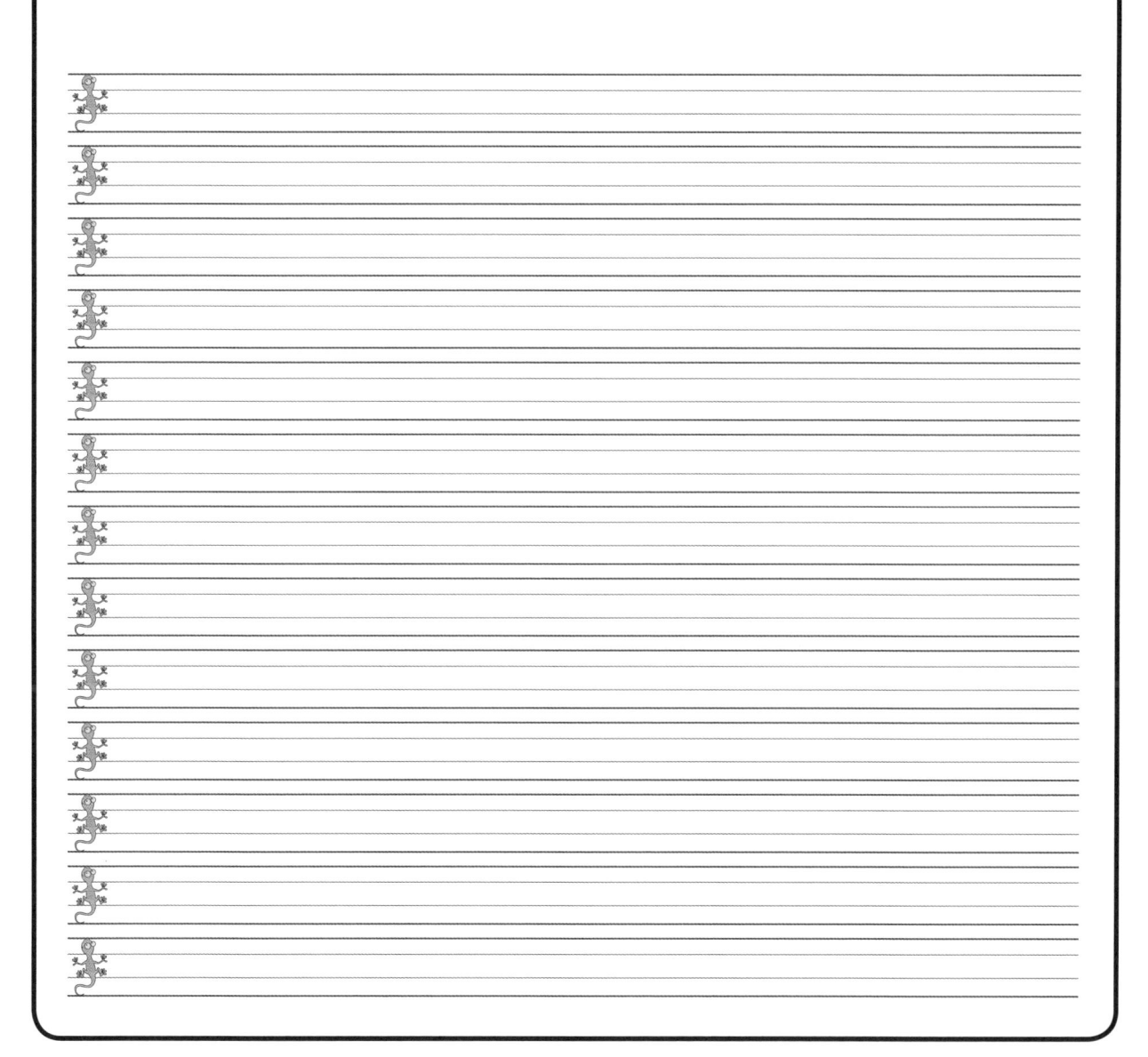

Chapter 3

Prefixes for negation (1)

Objective

To practise writing words with the prefixes for negation 'il-', 'ir-' and 'in-'.

Background knowledge

In this section, the children use the following negative prefixes: 'il-', 'ir-' and 'in-'. Point out that there is no adjustment made for double letters, for example 'il' + 'literate' becomes 'illiterate', 'ir' + 'regular' becomes 'irregular'. The prefixes 'il-' and 'ir-' are only used as prefixes when joining to words that begin with the last letter of the prefix, 'l' and 'r'.

The most common negative prefixes are 'in-' and 'un-'. Unfortunately, there is no rule to work out which one to use. The best way is to become familiar with them through use.

When joining from 'il-' the children practise the end-low diagonal join. When joining from 'ir-' the children practise the end-high horizontal join. When joining from 'in-' the children practise the end-low drop-on join to 'e', 'a', and c, and the end-low diagonal join to 'v'.

Left-handers may wish to lift their pen from the paper while joining, thus avoiding having to push awkwardly across the page. If the ink or pencil trace disappears, do not tell them they have to produce a joining mark. However, do ensure they are joining just above the paper, rather than printing. Left-handers may also want to produce a sharper, more italic-style exit to their end-low joins. This is fine as long as they leave enough space between their words and don't cramp their letters together.

Activities

● **Photocopiable page 71 'Which uses the 'il-' prefix?'**
In this activity, children are given a list of eight words and select which ones take the 'il-' prefix when used as a negative. There are four red herrings that use the 'un-' or 'dis-' prefix (likely, lawful, ladylike, like). When joining from 'il-' the children practise the end-low diagonal join to 'l'. They practise the joins by writing the negative words into one box and the red herrings into another. They then have more practice by using the negative words in sentences of their own.

● **Photocopiable page 72 'The 'ir-' prefix'**
The focus here is the prefix 'ir-'. The join between 'i' and 'r' is an end-low diagonal join, and the join from 'r' is an end-high diagonal or drop-on join, depending on the following letter. In this activity, children are given six words that can be changed into negative words by adding the 'ir-' prefix. They are asked to rewrite them to give their opposite meanings, and then reorganise them into alphabetical order and give their definitions.

● **Photocopiable page 73 'The 'in-' prefix'**
During this activity, the children practise the end-low drop-on join by joining the 'in-' prefix to root words beginning with 'a' and 'c'. You might like to discuss the last sentence of this activity with the children and point out that the word 'exclude' already has a prefix, which must be removed before adding the 'in-' prefix.

Further ideas

● **Writing tools:** Provide the children with different writing mediums, such as ballpoint pens, felt-tipped pens, crayons and chalk. Ask them to write the words from the activities to experiment with the effect each medium has on their handwriting.

What's on the CD-ROM

On the CD-ROM you will find:
● Animation of the joins.
● All of the photocopiable pages.

Prefixes for negation (1)

Which uses the 'il-' prefix?

- Use the prefix 'il-' to turn some of these words into the opposite meaning. Take care! There are some red herrings.
- Write the 'il-' negatives in one box and the red herrings in the other.

literate   logical   likely   legal   lawful   ladylike   liberal   like

'il-' opposites	Red herrings

- Now use the 'il-' words in sentences of your own.

Chapter 3

Prefixes for negation (1)

The 'ir-' prefix

■ Add the 'ir-' prefix to give these adjectives their opposite meaning.

~~responsible~~   regular   rational   replaceable   relevant   resistible

irresponsible

■ Organise the new words into alphabetical order and write a definition for each one.

Prefixes for negation (1)

The 'in-' prefix

- Read the sentences and rewrite them with the opposite meaning using 'in-'.
- Take care with the last sentence.

1. The measurements were exact.

2. Your drawing of the church was accurate.

3. She shows a great ability to concentrate.

4. I think the lunch today is edible.

5. That particular illness is curable.

6. I think that password is valid.

7. The group will exclude anyone without a ticket.

Chapter 3

Prefixes for negation (2)

Objective

To practise writing words with the prefixes for negation, 'im-', 'non-' and 'anti-'.

Background knowledge

The 'im-' prefix is most often used for words beginning with 'm' or 'p' to give the opposite meaning, such as 'immature' and 'impatient'.

The prefix 'non-', meaning 'not', doesn't have any rules governing its use, but it is commonly used with nouns, for example 'nonsense', 'nonentity'.

The 'anti-' prefix originates from Greek, meaning 'against' or 'in opposition'. Sometimes it may be hyphenated, for example 'anti-war'. Familiarity with these prefixes is best learned through usage. Explain that the prefix 'anti-' should not be confused with the prefix 'ante-', which means 'before'. You might point out that sometimes a hyphen is needed to avoid confusion or to separate two vowels to help pronunciation, for example 'anti-imperialism', or when a proper noun follows the prefix, for example 'anti-Europe'.

Left-handers may wish to lift their pen from the paper while joining, thus avoiding having to push awkwardly across the page. If the ink or pencil trace disappears, do not tell them they have to produce a joining mark. However, do ensure they are joining just above the paper, rather than printing. Left-handers may also want to produce a sharper, more italic-style exit to their end-low joins. This is fine as long as they leave enough space between their words and don't cramp their letters together.

Activities

- **Photocopiable page 75 'Negatives using 'im-"**
The focus here is the prefix 'im-'. Joining 'i' to 'm' is an end-low diagonal join. In this activity, children rewrite sentences and change the emboldened word to give the sentence the opposite meaning. Point out that no adjustment should be made for double consonants, such as 'immature'. The children practise the end-low diagonal join to the letters 'p' and 'm'.

- **Photocopiable page 76 'Words beginning with 'non-"**
In this activity, children practise a variety of joins, draw attention to where the second style of 'e' and 's' are needed. They are given a list of words beginning with 'non-' and asked to write a sentence for each of the words. Children may need to check the meanings with a dictionary before they begin.

- **Photocopiable page 77 "Anti-"**
When writing the prefix 'anti-' the children will be practising end-low diagonal joins. If followed by an end-low drop-on letter, such as 'c', remind the children to go from the writing line to 1 o'clock and then start the next letter. In this activity, children copy words beginning with the 'anti-' prefix and write a definition, having checked the words with a dictionary. They are then given six more words to change into the opposite using the 'anti-' prefix.

Further ideas

- **Prefixes rule!:** Encourage the children to describe rules for adding each of the prefixes. Create a word wall with the rules written on it. Children add words to the wall that fit each of the rules as they encounter them.

What's on the CD-ROM

On the CD-ROM you will find:
- Animation of the joins.
- All of the photocopiable pages.

Scholastic Literacy Skills
Handwriting: Years 5–6

Name: Chapter 3

Prefixes for negation (2)

Negatives using 'im-'

■ Rewrite these sentences to have the opposite meaning by changing the word in bold into a negative word with the prefix 'im-'.

1. Getting there on time is **possible**.

2. The younger children are being very **mature** today.

3. The aliens on Planet Zorg are all **mortal** beings.

4. I'm sure that boulder on the footpath is **moveable**.

5. My teacher was very **patient** yesterday.

6. **Perfection** is sometimes a good thing in a painting.

7. He was **polite** to the visitors.

8. Rain for our sports day is highly **probable**.

9. The map was too **precise** to help them escape.

SCHOLASTIC   PHOTOCOPIABLE   Scholastic Literacy Skills
www.scholastic.co.uk   Handwriting: Years 5–6   75

Chapter 3 Name:

Prefixes for negation (2)
Words beginning with 'non-'

■ Write a sentence for each of these words. Use a dictionary to check the meaning.

1. nonsense

2. non-existent

3. non-fiction

4. non-payment

5. non-stop

6. nondescript

Name: Chapter 3

Prefixes for negation (2)

'Anti-'

■ The prefix 'anti-', when added to a word, changes the word's meaning to show the opposite, or opposition to something, or being against something. Sometimes it is used with a hyphen, as in 'anti-war'.

■ Copy these words, look them up in a dictionary and write a definition for each one.

1. antiseptic   meaning

   antiseptic

2. anticlimax   meaning

3. antibiotic   meaning

4. antisocial   meaning

■ Now add a prefix to the following words to change their meaning to show the opposite. Use a dictionary to check if they need a hyphen.

bullying _____   aircraft _____

government _____   virus _____

smoking _____   clockwise _____

Chapter 3

Words with a Latin root (1)

Objective

To practise writing words using prefixes and word roots with Latin roots, 'prim-', 'aqua-' and 'multi-'.

Background knowledge

The English language borrows many words, including prefixes, from Ancient Greek and Latin. An understanding of their meanings will help children understand and work out the meaning of words. The prefix 'prim-' means 'first' or 'early', 'aqua-' relates the word to water, while 'multi-' means 'many' or 'more than one'. When forming the join, remind children to finish the letter first before travelling from the end of the letter to the start of the next. This will avoid the letters sitting on top of each other.

Left-handers may wish to lift their pen from the paper while joining, thus avoiding having to push awkwardly across the page. If the ink or pencil trace disappears, do not tell them they have to produce a joining mark. However, do ensure they are joining just above the paper, rather than printing. Left-handers may also want to produce a sharper, more italic-style exit to their end-low joins. This is fine as long as they leave enough space between their words and don't cramp their letters together.

Activities

- **Photocopiable page 79 'First things first'**
In this activity, children write their own definitions for six words beginning with the word root 'prim-'. Before beginning, ask the children what 'prim' means at the start of a word and explain if needed. They then check the definitions and use each word in a sentence. The children practise a range of joins, including end-low diagonal and end-high horizontal in the word root 'prim-'. Be careful to check the join from 'r' to 'i' is not too high as this can be a common mistake.

- **Photocopiable page 80 'Water'**
In this activity, children write and define five words that begin with the word root 'aqua-'. They check the definitions with a dictionary and then make up four new 'aqua-' words. When forming the join from 'q', encourage children to finish the letter first before travelling from the end of the letter straight up to the start of the next. This will avoid a gap between the 'q' and 'u' that is too large.

- **Photocopiable page 81 'More than one'**
The focus here is the 'multi-' root, which is made up of end-low diagonal joins. In this activity, children choose words from a word bank to fill the gaps in sentences. Check that the children understand the meaning of the prefix before they start. As they are writing, the children will practise the end-low diagonal join and the end-low drop-on join.

Further ideas

- **Latin origins:** Encourage the children to collect and practise writing other words with Latin origins from other curriculum areas (for example, science, geography and numeracy).
- **Greek origins:** Suggest that the children research examples of words that use word roots of Greek origin and compare them with Latin words.

What's on the CD-ROM

On the CD-ROM you will find:
- Animation of the joins.
- All of the photocopiable pages.

Name: Chapter 3

Words with a Latin root (1)

First things first

■ Words that begin with the word root 'prim-' have meanings that relate to 'first' or 'early'.

■ What do you think these words mean? Write each word in the first column and add your own definition in the next column.

> primary   prime   primarily   primitive   primal   primate

■ Check your definitions with a dictionary. Then use some words in sentences.

Chapter 3   Name:

Words with a Latin root (1)

Water

- The word root 'aqua-' is used to relate something to water.
- What do you think these words mean? Write the word in the first column and add your own definition in the next column.

| aquarium   aquamarine   aquaplane   aquatic   aqualung |

- Make up three new words of your own that could relate to water by adding the 'aqua-' root. Here's one to start you off.

aqua + scooter

Scholastic Literacy Skills
Handwriting: Years 5–6

PHOTOCOPIABLE
www.scholastic.co.uk

Words with a Latin root (1)

More than one

- Words that use 'multi-' mean 'many' or 'more than one'.
- Choose a word to complete each sentence and write it in the space.

| multicultural | multisyllabic | multicoloured |
| multimedia | multimillionaires | multiply |

1. A rainbow is a _____ arch shape in the sky.

2. If you _____ seven by seven you get forty-nine.

3. 'Multimedia' is a _____ word.

4. A combination of ways to present content, such as text, audio, video and interactivity, is known as _____ .

5. When people of many races live and work together, they belong to a _____ society .

6. Many rich pop stars and musicians are _____ .

Chapter 3

Words with a Latin root (2)

Objective

To practise writing words using prefixes and word roots with Latin roots, 'quad-', 'auto-' and 'mari-'.

Background knowledge

Knowing the meaning of a prefix or word root can help children work out the meaning of new words and help with spelling. The prefix 'quad-' has a Latin origin and relates to the number four.

The prefix 'auto-' changes the root word to meaning 'of or by oneself or itself' as in 'autobiography'. The children practise a variety of joins depending on the first letter of the root word, including the end-high horizontal join and the end-high diagonal join to the letter 'b'.

The word root 'mari-' comes from Latin, meaning 'of the sea' or 'of water'.

Left-handers may wish to lift their pen from the paper while joining, thus avoiding having to push awkwardly across the page. If the ink or pencil trace disappears, do not tell them they have to produce a joining mark. However, do ensure they are joining just above the paper, rather than printing. Left-handers may also want to produce a sharper, more italic-style exit. This is fine as long as they leave enough space between their words and don't cramp their letters together.

Activities

● **Photocopiable page 83 'Quads'**
In this activity, children work with the 'quad-' prefix, (which consists of end-low diagonal and drop-on joins) to match the word to the statements. When forming the join from 'q', encourage children to finish the letter first before travelling from the end of the letter straight up to the start of the next. This will avoid a gap between the 'q' and 'u' that is too large. The letter which follows 'quad-' is always an 'r' which the children will use an end-low diagonal join for.

● **Photocopiable page 84 'Auto'**
The focus here is the 'auto-' prefix, which uses end-low diagonal and end-low drop-on joins. When adding it to a word, the children will need to use an end-high join from the letter 'o'. In this activity, children copy the words and write their own definitions before checking with a dictionary. Once they understand the meanings, they complete sentences where a word using the prefix is missing. Remind the children that 't' is a shorter head letter and to cross the letter once they have written the word in full.

● **Photocopiable page 85 'Something watery'**
In this activity, children work with the word root 'mari-', which consists of end-low drop-on, end-low diagonal and end-high horizontal joins. Ensure the children have a full understanding of how prefixes work as they will need to write an explanation of how the prefix is used. Remind the children that they will need to use the second style of 'e' in these 'mari-' words.

Further ideas

● **Numbers:** Suggest that the children find other prefixes that relate to numbers. Create a word wall for each prefix and encourage the children to write the words they discover, with their meanings, and add them to the wall.
● **Writing prefixes:** Ask the children to collect other words with Latin prefixes from shared and guided reading and use them in writing sentences.

What's on the CD-ROM

On the CD-ROM you will find:
● Animation of the joins.
● All of the photocopiable pages.

Name: Chapter 3

Words with a Latin root (2)

Quads

■ Which word best fits each of these descriptions?

> quadrangle   quadrilateral   quadruple   quadruped   quadruplets

1. A flat shape with four straight sides.

2. An animal with four feet.

3. This can be a four-sided shape or a square courtyard.

4. Four siblings born at the same time.

5. To make something four times as big.

■ Now write five sentences to show how each word can be used.

PHOTOCOPIABLE

Scholastic Literacy Skills
Handwriting: Years 5–6   83

Chapter 3   Name:

Words with a Latin root (2)

Auto

■ These words all begin with the prefix 'auto-'.
■ Write each word and your own definition. Then check the definitions with a dictionary.

autonomous

autonomous

automatic

autobiography

autographs

automated

autopilot

■ Which word is missing from these sentences? Write them in the spaces.

1. He turned off the _____ to land the plane.

2. I have done it so often it has become _____ .

3. I collect the _____ of my favourite stars.

4. An _____ is a person's story of their own life.

5. The factory uses fully _____ machinery.

6. Each group will be _____ during the project.

Scholastic Literacy Skills
84 Handwriting: Years 5–6

PHOTOCOPIABLE

SCHOLASTIC
www.scholastic.co.uk

Name: Chapter 3

Words with a Latin root (2)

Something watery

■ Find out the meaning of these words.

| marine   marinate   mariner   maritime   marinade   marina |

■ Write each word and definition.

■ Write an explanation of how to use the prefix 'mari-'.

Chapter 4
Common letter strings

Introduction

This chapter focuses on writing words with common letter strings. The first section focuses on suffixes, specifically the 'shun' sound ending ('-tion' and '-sion' are commonly used to change verbs into nouns, whereas '-cian' is commonly used to change a verb into the name of a profession).

The next section focuses on the letter 'c' followed by a vowel, differentiating between hard and soft 'c' sounds. The children then practise using connectives to link sentences and phrases. In the following section, they practise writing words with common letter strings but different pronunciations, 'ear', 'ie' and 'ough'.

The children will continue to practise a wide variety of joins in the activities and their understanding of the words used in this chapter is emphasised in each activity.

In this chapter

Different spelling, same sound page 87	To practise writing words with suffixes '-cian', '-tion' and '-sion'.
The letter 'c' page 91	To practise joining from the letter 'c'.
Connectives page 95	To practise writing and using connecting words and phrases.
Same spelling, different sound page 99	To practise writing words with the same spelling but different sounds, 'ear', 'ie' and 'ough'.
Word families page 103	To practise writing words that are grouped as families of words with letters 'ctu', 'tch' and 'gue'.

Different spelling, same sound

Objective

To practise writing words with suffixes '-cian', '-tion' and '-sion'.

Background knowledge

Suffixes ending in '-ion' give the most common spelling for words that end with the 'shun' sound. The spelling of the suffix depends on the spelling of the root word. Most words ending in '-cian' are words used to name a job or profession. The suffix '-tion' is the most used and changes the root word from a verb into a noun, sometimes altering the root word's spelling. The suffix '-sion' also changes the root word from a verb into a noun and is used with words ending in 'd', 'de', 's' and 'se'.

When adding '-sion' to a word using a double 's', remind the children that they will both be the second style of 's'. Remind the children that they do not need to go over to the drop on. Instead, end low, curve up and stop when they hit the top of the body. They then draw their pencil slightly back down the stroke they have just made before forming the bottom curl of the 's'.

Left-handers may wish to lift their pen from the paper while joining, thus avoiding having to push awkwardly across the page. If the ink or pencil trace disappears, do not tell them they have to produce a joining mark. However, do ensure they are joining just above the paper, rather than printing. Left-handers may also want to produce a sharper, more italic-style exit to their end-low joins. This is fine as long as they leave enough space between their words and don't cramp their letters together.

Activities

- **Photocopiable page 88 'What am I?'**
The focus of this activity is the suffix '-cian'. A number of joins are practised, especially the drop-on join to 'c' and 'a' and the end-low diagonal join from 'c' to 'i' and 'a' to 'n'. The children need to work out the names of professions and then write down any other professions they know ending in '-cian' on the word web.
- **Photocopiable page 89 'Verbs to nouns (4)'**
Using the '-tion' suffix, the children practise the end-low diagonal, end-low drop-on and the end-high horizontal joins. They must change verbs to nouns by adding '-tion' to the root word. Discuss the verbs to check the children understand that some spellings need to be changed before adding the suffix. They then sort the words according to how the root word changes.
- **Photocopiable page 90 'Verbs to nouns (5)'**
The children fill in missing nouns in sentences, all using the '-sion' suffix. The suffix will practise forming the second style of 's', end-low diagonal, end-low drop-on and end-high horizontal joins. The children use the word bank of verbs provided and change them into nouns. It would help them to go through the verbs first and explore how the root words change before the addition of the suffix.

Further ideas

- **Word wall:** Create a word wall for each of the suffixes. Encourage the children to add to the wall when they encounter relevant words.
- **Dictionaries:** Ask the children to use a dictionary to find as many words as they can containing the suffixes and write them down, inside a given time. Compare the results and the handwriting legibility.

What's on the CD-ROM

On the CD-ROM you will find:
- Animation of the joins.
- All of the photocopiable pages.

Chapter 4 — Name:

Different spelling, same sound

What am I?

■ Write the profession to complete these sentences.

1. Beauty is my trade. I am a _____.
2. If you need a change of diet, I will work one out for you. I am a _____.
3. I work in politics. I am a _____.
4. I love music and want to be a _____.
5. I am involved in technical work. I am a _____.
6. If the electrics don't work, I call out an _____.

■ Can you think of any other professions or jobs that end in the suffix '-cian'? Write them below.

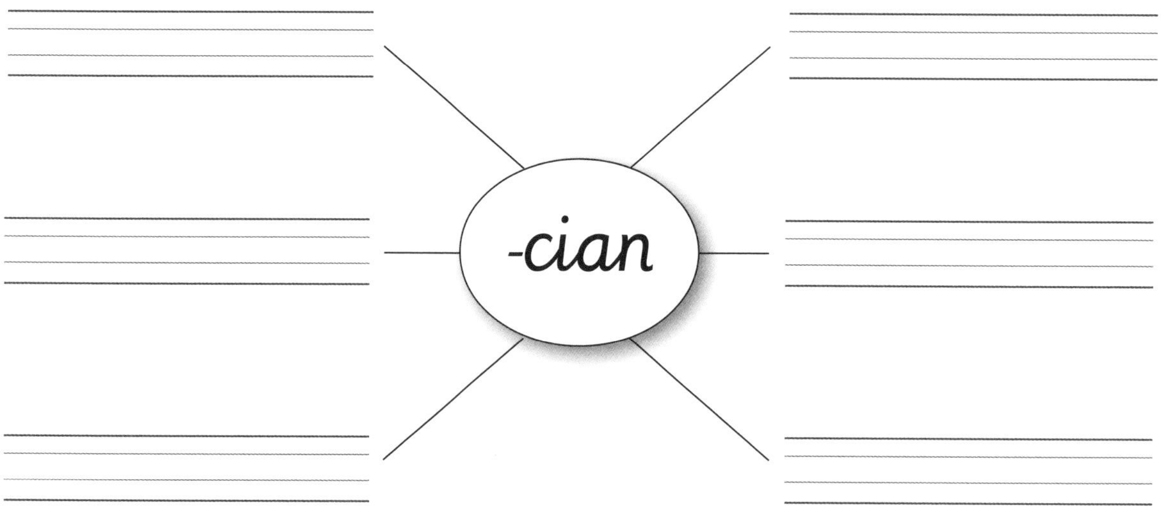

-cian

Scholastic Literacy Skills
Handwriting: Years 5–6

PHOTOCOPIABLE
www.scholastic.co.uk

Different spelling, same sound

Name: Chapter 4

Verbs to nouns (4)

- Change these verbs into nouns by adding the '-tion' suffix.
- Take care, some verbs need to have the spelling of the root word changed.

Verb		Noun
abbreviate	=	
revolve	=	
occupy	=	
fascinate	=	
quote	=	
react	=	
describe	=	
hibernate	=	
solve	=	
imitate	=	

- Group the words below according to how the root word changes.

Drop the 'e' and add '-tion'	Change the ending of the root word	Just add '-tion'

Chapter 4

Different spelling, same sound

Name:

Verbs to nouns (5)

■ Complete the sentences using nouns ending in '-sion'. Use the verbs in the word bank to help you.

| divide   erode   submit   collide   revise   include   decide   confuse |

1. The river bank is suffering from _____ after the high tides.

2. He always struggles with _____ in the numeracy class.

3. The _____ to add salad to the menu has been well received.

4. The competition closes today and no _____ will be accepted after 3pm.

5. I am going to do lots of _____ before the test this time.

6. I hope his _____ in the team will mean we play better.

7. Just so there is no _____, I'll go through the rules once more.

8. The bus driver narrowly avoided a bad _____ this morning.

Scholastic Literacy Skills
90 Handwriting: Years 5–6

PHOTOCOPIABLE

SCHOLASTIC
www.scholastic.co.uk

The letter 'c'

Objective

To practise joining from the letter 'c'.

Background knowledge

The letter 'c' has a wide variety of pronunciations. The differing sounds come from the origin of the words – hard 'c' for words that come from German origin, and soft 'c' for words of French origin. Pronunciation of words containing 'c' followed by a vowel can be either hard as in 'cat', or soft as in 'lace'. When 'c' is followed by the letter 'y', the 'c' sound is soft, as in 'cynic'.

When the 'c' occurs in the middle of the word, the children practise the drop-on join to 'c'. Remind the children that the join takes them to where the next letter starts. In this case, the start of the drop-on letter is over at 1 o'clock, not 12 o'clock. Remind the children that when joining 'c' to 'e' they will form the second style of 'e' and need to go to the middle of the clock before going round to 1 o'clock.

Left-handers may wish to lift their pen from the paper while joining, thus avoiding having to push awkwardly across the page. If the ink or pencil trace disappears, do not tell them they have to produce a joining mark. However, do ensure they are joining just above the paper, rather than printing. Left-handers may also want to produce a sharper, more italic-style exit to their end-low joins. This is fine as long as they leave enough space between their words and don't cramp their letters together.

Activities

● **Photocopiable page 92 'Hard or soft?'**
The children practise using the drop-on join to 'c' and the end-low diagonal and drop-on joins from 'c'. They practise further joins by adding more words from their own knowledge and think of a rule for pronunciation. They are given ten words that contain the letter 'c' followed by the vowels 'a' and 'i'. Ask the children to read the words aloud before they sort the words into 'hard c' or 'soft c'.

● **Photocopiable page 93 "cy' wordsearch'**
In this activity, the children look for seven words in a wordsearch grid. The seven words to find all contain the 'cy' letter string (lacy, fancy, cycle, cygnet, cynic, cylinder, mercy). They practise writing the end-low diagonal join from 'c' to 'y' by writing the words below the grid when they find them, and formulate a rule for pronouncing words with the 'cy' spelling. Before the activity, warn the children to look out for red herring 'c' words.

● **Photocopiable page 94 "ce' and 'co' words'**
The children are given 12 words with the 'ce' or 'co' letter strings. Remind them that 'e' after 'c' will be the second style. They practise writing the words using the end-low diagonal join to 'e' and the drop-on join to 'o'. They group the words into two spaces according to either the hard or soft 'c' sound. One word, 'ocean', doesn't conform to the pattern, it has a 'sh' sound.

Further ideas

● **Shhh:** Challenge the children to find words where 'c' has the 'sh' sound (such as 'conscious'). See how many they can write in a list. You could time the activity and see if they manage to retain a neat style.

● **Eyes closed:** Ask the children to write a word from this section, then close their eyes and write it again underneath. Are there any differences between the two words? Ask them to repeat the task, but this time write exactly on top of the first word.

What's on the CD-ROM

On the CD-ROM you will find:
● Animation of the joins.
● All of the photocopiable pages.

Chapter 4   Name:

The letter 'c'

Hard or soft?

- Which words have a soft 'c' sound and which words have a hard 'c' sound?
- Write the words into the correct shape.

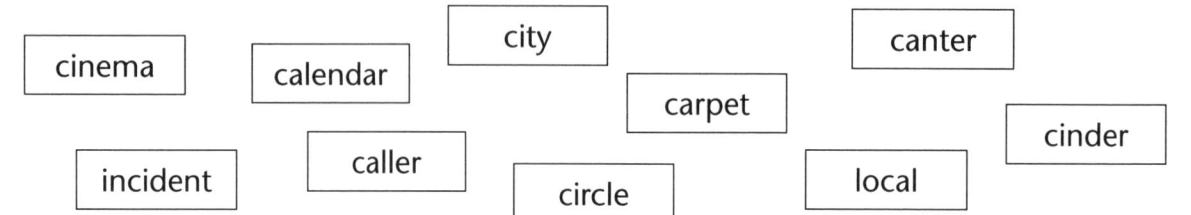

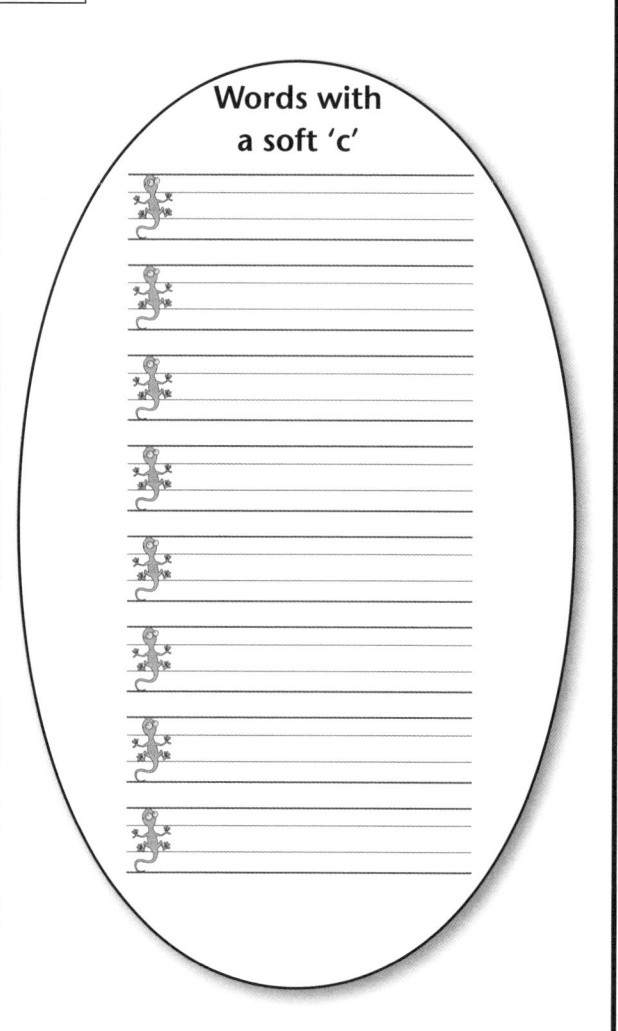

cinema   calendar   city   carpet   canter   cinder

incident   caller   circle   local

Words with a hard 'c'

Words with a soft 'c'

- Think of three more hard 'c' words and three more soft 'c' words and add them to the shapes.

- Can you think of a rule for saying words when 'c' is followed by 'a' and 'i'?

Name: Chapter 4

The letter 'c'

'cy' wordsearch

- Hidden in the grid are seven words containing the letters 'cy'.
- Find the words and write them underneath.

c	u	b	e	c	m	f	e
r	b	o	f	y	e	c	k
y	i	c	a	l	r	c	h
g	c	y	n	i	c	a	t
d	y	g	c	n	y	t	a
a	c	n	y	d	b	n	c
l	l	e	a	e	h	e	y
b	e	t	t	r	a	c	y
p	l	a	c	y	q	r	s

- Write a rule to show how 'cy' words are pronounced.

_____
_____
_____
_____
_____

PHOTOCOPIABLE

Scholastic Literacy Skills
Handwriting: Years 5–6

93

Chapter 4 Name:

The letter 'c'

'ce' and 'co' words

- Which words have a soft 'c' sound and which words have a hard 'c' sound?
- Write the words into the correct shape.

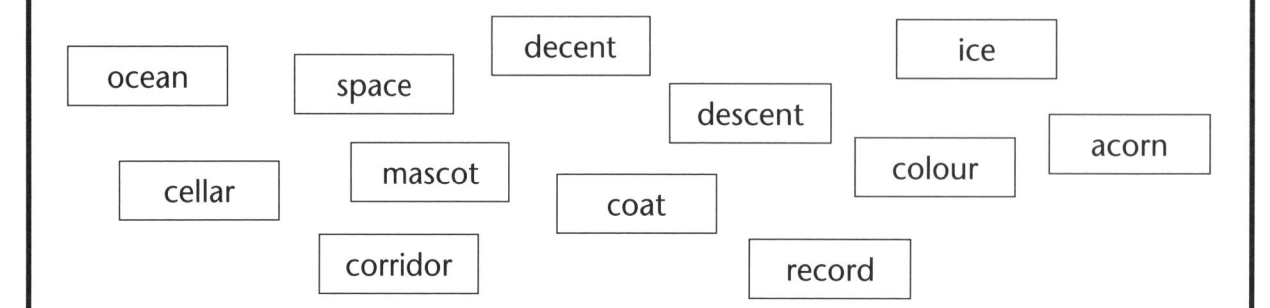

ocean   space   decent   ice
   cellar   mascot   descent   colour   acorn
      corridor   coat   record

Hard sound

Soft sound

- Which word is the odd one out? Why?

The odd one out is _____ because _____

Chapter 4

Connectives

Objective

To practise writing and using connecting words and phrases.

Background knowledge

Connectives are words and phrases used to link clauses and sentences. They can be conjunctions, adverbs or adverbial phrases and have a variety of uses, including extending an idea, making comparisons, giving opposing ideas, contrasts, showing cause and effect or showing a sequence and the passage of time.

They are used to allow writing to flow and help the reader understand links between ideas or the sequence of events.

Left-handers may wish to lift their pen from the paper while joining, thus avoiding having to push awkwardly across the page. If the ink or pencil trace disappears, do not tell them they have to produce a joining mark. However, do ensure they are joining just above the paper, rather than printing. Left-handers may also want to produce a sharper, more italic-style exit to their end-low joins. This is fine as long as they leave enough space between their words and don't cramp their letters together.

Activities

- **Photocopiable page 96 'Single-word connectives'**
The children are given a word bank of single-word connectives. They choose connectives to make sense of sentences and write them in the gaps. Children have the opportunity to practise a variety of joins while writing the words. Remind them that 'x' can be joined if they wish, but if they are finding it tricky, they do not have to join it. Also remind them to dot the 'i's and cross the 't's when the finish writing the word.

- **Photocopiable page 97 'Connecting phrases'**
In this activity, children are given a choice of two connecting phrases to use within a specified context. They write the two phrases and then choose which is the best connective to use by giving the one they prefer a tick. Some choices are more obvious than others, but sometimes personal preference should be allowed. Children have the opportunity to practise a variety of joins while writing the words. Remind them that there should be equal spacing between the words. They then write out the whole sentence or sentences.

- **Photocopiable page 98 'Compound connectives'**
A list of simple words that can be combined to form connectives is provided. The children experiment with putting them together to see how many different connectives they can make. The children have the opportunity to practise a variety of joins while writing the words. Remind them that the two words should be combined to form a complete word with even spacing between each letter.

Further ideas

- **Connective pairs:** Provide groups with a collection of word cards, face down. Ask them to pick two words and put them together as a connective. When they are all used up, ask them to write down the ones that actually are connectives and discard the others.
- **Joining:** Provide the children with large sheets of paper and different writing mediums to practise the joins, such as salt (by pouring), paint or water (in squeezy bottles). Encourage them to practise writing connectives using large hand/arm movements.

What's on the CD-ROM

On the CD-ROM you will find:
- Tramline practice areas for all three activities.
- All of the photocopiable pages.

Scholastic Literacy Skills
Handwriting: Years 5–6

Connectives

Single-word connectives

■ Choose a connective from the word bank to fill in each gap and make sense of these sentences.

> despite   later   firstly   but   although   since   fortunately   next

1. We spent the afternoon in the park. _____ we went to the cinema.

2. The rain poured down. _____ we had umbrellas with us.

3. We really had fun, _____ the awful weather.

4. Follow this recipe carefully. _____ you must prepare the ingredients.

5. _____ she had flu, she has felt really weak and tired.

6. I enjoy classical music _____ I really like pop more!

7. He ran as fast as he could _____ he realised he wouldn't win.

8. Crack two eggs. _____ beat them in a bowl with a dash of milk.

Name: _____   Chapter 4

Connectives

Connecting phrases

■ Some connectives to link sentences and ideas are made by using a phrase, that is, two or more words. They are used to help your writing flow and help your reader understand links between ideas or the sequence of events.
■ Try out both phrases below by writing each one in the gap.
■ Choose the best phrase and give the one you prefer a tick.
■ Then write the sentence or sentences out in full.

1. Team A made good time across the field. _____
   team B set off through the wood.
   Team A made good time across the field. _____
   team B set off through the wood.
   ☐ In the meantime,
   ☐ On the other hand,

2. I don't like climbing. _____ I won't be going on
   the climbing trip.
   I don't like climbing. _____ I won't be going on
   the climbing trip.
   ☐ In other words,
   ☐ For this reason,

3. We reached the adventure park _____ the bus
   broke down.
   We reached the adventure park _____ the bus
   broke down.
   ☐ just as
   ☐ all at once

Connectives

Compound connectives

■ Some connectives are made by joining two or more shorter words together, for example more + over = moreover

■ Put two or more of the words together to make connectives. How many can you make?

	how	where	ever	further	more	there	for
over	mean	while	what	be	sides	by	never	the
		less	when	none	who	as		

■ Write your connectives in a list.

Same spelling, different sound

Objective

To practise writing words with the same spelling but different sounds, 'ear', 'ie' and 'ough'.

Background knowledge

There are many words in English that share the same letter strings but have different sounds.

The letter string 'ear' is most commonly pronounced in two ways: 'air' as in 'pear', and 'eer' as in 'deer'. But it can also be pronounced in other ways, such as 'er' as in 'learn' and 'ar' as in 'heart'.

The letter string 'ie' is also most commonly pronounced in two ways: long sounds 'eye' and 'ee'. However there are other variations, such as a short 'e' sound ('friend') and separating the sounds ('diet', 'alien').

The letter string 'ough' has the widest variety of pronunciations in the English language. This letter string can be pronounced in a total of nine commonly used ways, though we only use seven of them normally: 'though', 'rough', 'cough', 'plough', 'through', 'thorough' and 'thought'; there is also 'hiccough' (or 'hiccup') and 'lough' (or 'loch').

Left-handers may wish to lift their pen from the paper while joining, thus avoiding having to push awkwardly across the page. If the ink or pencil trace disappears, do not tell them they have to produce a joining mark. However, do ensure they are joining just above the paper, rather than printing.

Activities

- **Photocopiable page 100 'What can you hear?'**
Twenty words containing the 'ear' letter string are provided for the children to sort. They practise forming the second style of 'e' in a medial position, as well as the tricky end-high onto 'e' join from 're' and end-high diagonal joins from 'r' to 'l'. There are three pronunciations of the letter string. Encourage the children to say each word and listen carefully to the sound before writing it in the correct container. Some words may be used in more than one container ('tear').

- **Photocopiable page 101 "ie' sounds'**
In this activity, children are given 15 words that share the 'ie' letter string. Joins practised include end-low diagonal and end-high horizontal joins. They also practise using the second style of 'e'. There are four ways to pronounce the letter string and the children sort the words into containers according to the sound made. Encourage them to say the words aloud before sorting them.

- **Photocopiable page 102 "ough' sounds'**
The children copy five sentences containing 12 emboldened words with the letter string 'ough'. They use six different pronunciations. The children then copy the words into a chart according to the different ways they are pronounced. Encourage them to read the sentences aloud before adding the 'ough' words to the chart. They have the opportunity to practise a variety of joining strokes while writing, including the drop-on joins to 'o' and 'g' and the end-high horizontal join from 'o' to 'u'.

Further ideas

- **Poem couplets:** Challenge the children to write short poems of rhyming couplets using the letter strings in these activities.
- **Word family chain:** Provide the children with a single 'ough' word, for example 'rough'. Ask them to write the word on a piece of paper, and then form a word family chain by adding suffixes. Limit the time allowed for the activity, and compare the results.

What's on the CD-ROM

On the CD-ROM you will find:
- Animation of the joins.
- All of the photocopiable pages.

Chapter 4 — Name:

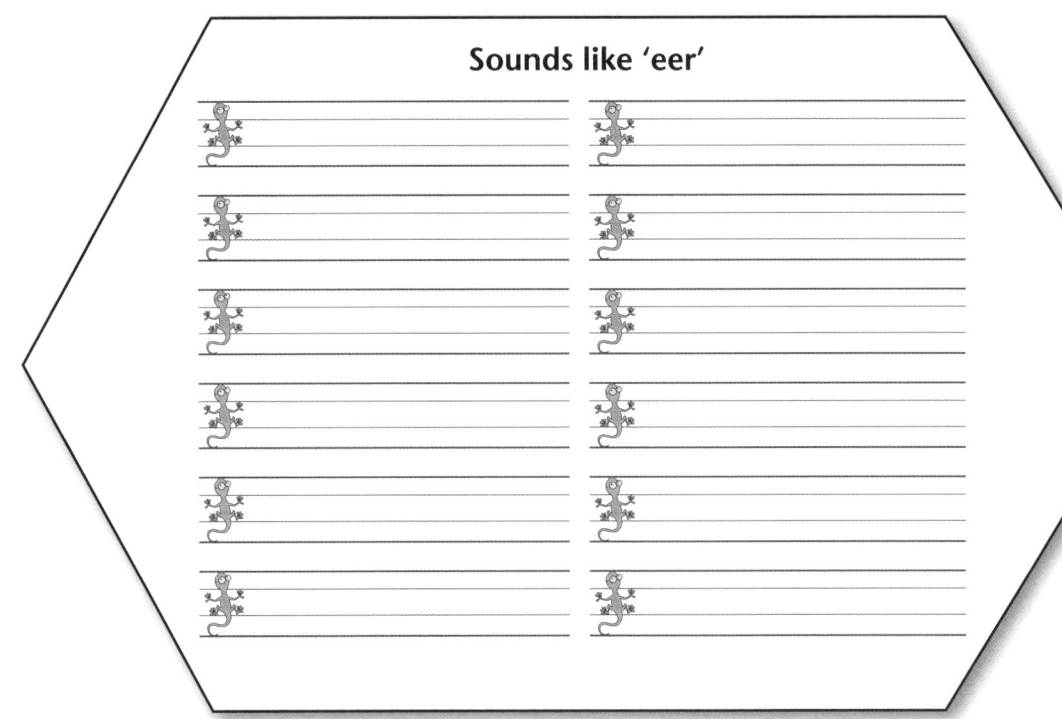

Same spelling, different sound

What can you hear?

■ These words all share the letter string 'ear'. Read them aloud and listen to how they are pronounced. Write the words into the 'sounds like' boxes.

| pear | tear | dear | earn | fear | learn | dreary | wear | weary | beard |
| early | bear | hear | clear | earth | gear | pearl | rear | search | spear |

Sounds like 'air'

Sounds like 'er'

Sounds like 'eer'

Scholastic Literacy Skills
Handwriting: Years 5–6

PHOTOCOPIABLE
www.scholastic.co.uk

Name: Chapter 4

Same spelling, different sound

'ie' sounds

■ These words all share the letter string 'ie'. Read them aloud and listen to how they are pronounced. Write the words into the 'sounds like' boxes.

> tie   diet   achieve   die   field   pie   alien
> ancient   friend   brief   lie   chief   fierce   fiery   flier

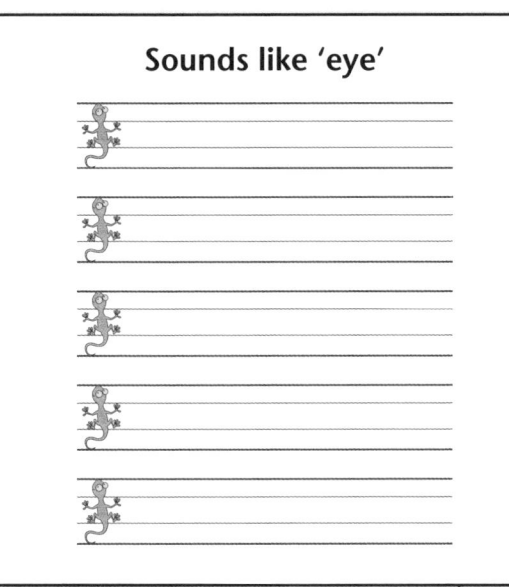

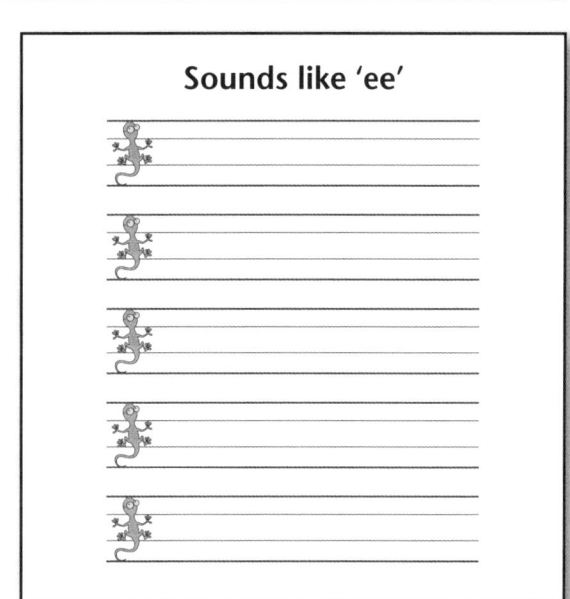

Sounds like 'eye'

Sounds like 'ee'

ie

Sounds like short 'e'

Two separate sounds

PHOTOCOPIABLE
www.scholastic.co.uk

Scholastic Literacy Skills
Handwriting: Years 5–6   101

Chapter 4 Name:

Same spelling, different sound

'ough' sounds

■ Copy these sentences.

1. **Although** I want to make pizza **dough**, I haven't **bought enough** flour.

2. The farmer's **plough** went **through** the field.

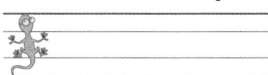

3. I **ought** to go to school but I have such a bad **cough**.

4. The hungry pigs didn't have **enough** food in their **trough**.

5. When Dad sawed the **bough** off the tree, it was a **tough** job.

■ Write the words into the grid to show how they are pronounced.

| although dough bought enough plough through |
| ought cough trough bough tough |

'oo' as in 'blue'	'ow' as in 'cow'	'ort' as in 'sort'

'o' as in 'toe'	'uff' as in 'stuff'	'off'

Scholastic Literacy Skills
Handwriting: Years 5–6

PHOTOCOPIABLE
SCHOLASTIC
www.scholastic.co.uk

Word families

Objective

To practise writing words that are grouped as families of words with letters 'ctu', 'tch' and 'gue'.

Background knowledge

Word families are collections of words that share common letter strings and are linked by meanings that are derived from a root word, for example 'family', 'familiarise', 'familiarity', 'unfamiliar'. They can be formed by adding prefixes and suffixes. Word families can also be sets of words that are linked by a common form of spelling, as in 'bright', 'light', 'sight', 'frighten' and so on.

The children practise a variety of joins in these activities. Remind them that the end-low drop-on join takes them to where the next letter starts. In this case, the start of the drop-on letter is over at 1 o'clock, not 12 o'clock. This formation avoids gaps in the top of the letter (for example making 'a' resemble 'u'; 'd' resemble 'cl'), or forcing the child to slant their letter backwards in order to close the top.

Left-handers may wish to lift their pen from the paper while joining, thus avoiding having to push awkwardly across the page. If the ink or pencil trace disappears, do not tell them they have to produce a joining mark. However, do ensure they are joining just above the paper, rather than printing. Left-handers may also want to produce a sharper, more italic-style exit to their end-low joins. This is fine as long as they leave enough space between their words and don't cramp their letters together.

Activities

- **Photocopiable page 104 "ctu' wordsearch'**
Six words with the letter string 'ctu' are hidden in the wordsearch (fracture, picture, nocturnal, lecture, actual, factual). While writing, the children practise the drop-on join to 'c' and the end-low diagonal join between 'c' and 't' and 'u'. They write the words as a list, then complete the sentences to demonstrate their understanding of the words. Warn the children to watch out for red herrings in the wordsearch.

- **Photocopiable page 105 'Word family spidergrams'**
In this activity, children are given four 'tch' words as the centre of four spidergrams. Encourage the children to add suffixes and prefixes to write words in the same family along the legs of each spidergram. Encourage them to add more legs if they can think of more words in the family. While they are writing they practise the drop-on join to 'c' and the end-low diagonal join.

- **Photocopiable page 106 "gue' word families'**
The children are given a list of eight words with the 'gue' spelling pattern and are asked to match them and then check the meaning with a dictionary. They then practise writing the words by using each one in a sentence of their own. While writing they are practising the end-low diagonal join and the drop-on join to 'e' – remind the children to start from the middle of the clock.

Further ideas

- **New words:** Using the words from photocopiable page 106 "gue' word families', encourage the children to experiment with adding suffixes to make new words, for example 'vagueness', 'roguery', 'guessing', or adding other words to make compound words, for example 'guestroom'.
- **Style:** Ask the children to write the same words or sentences on different types of surface using different writing implements. Talk about the different effects and which is easier, faster or more attractive.

What's on the CD-ROM

On the CD-ROM you will find:
- Animation of the joins.
- All of the photocopiable pages.

Chapter 4 Name:

Word families

'ctu' wordsearch

■ Hidden in the wordsearch are six words with the letter string 'ctu'.

a	c	t	p	c	c	t	u	l	p
b	t	u	i	t	t	w	k	e	c
f	r	a	c	t	u	r	e	c	t
a	p	c	t	u	p	y	c	t	u
c	c	t	u	p	r	c	t	u	z
t	u	u	r	g	s	t	u	r	f
u	c	a	e	m	c	t	u	e	b
a	b	l	g	c	t	v	c	t	u
l	n	o	c	t	u	r	n	a	l
x	o	c	t	u	v	s	p	w	h

■ Write the 'ctu' words in a list here.

■ Choose the correct word to fill the gap in each sentence.

1. A _____ description of an experience or an event is called a recount.

2. If you _____ a bone, you break it.

3. When I do something wrong, my mum gives me a _____ .

4. A badger is normally a _____ creature.

5. I have a _____ of some horses on my bedroom wall.

6. I thought he was 9 but his _____ age is 10.

Name:

Chapter 4

Word families
Word family spidergrams

■ Look at the root word in these spidergrams. How many new words from the same family can you add to the legs?

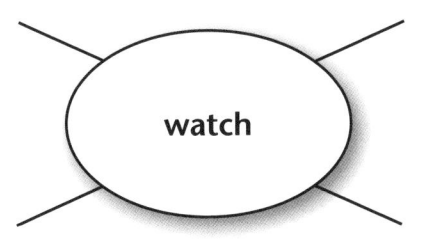

watch

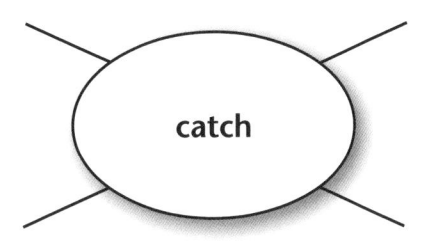

catch

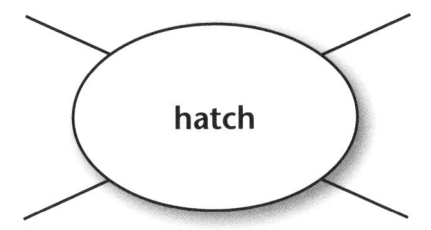

hatch

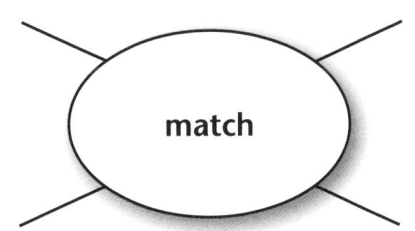

match

PHOTOCOPIABLE

Scholastic Literacy Skills
Handwriting: Years 5–6   105

Chapter 4 Name:

Word families

'gue' word families

■ Match these words to their meaning.

rogue	not clear
argue	an invited visitor
dialogue	give a rough idea
guess	a muscle in the mouth
vague	tiredness
tongue	conversation
fatigue	give reasons against something
guest	a deceitful person

■ Now use each word in a sentence.

Chapter 5
Refining handwriting

Introduction

This chapter focuses on refining handwriting and developing an individual style. People use different styles and sizes of handwriting for different purposes. Developing appropriate styles for the purpose and audience is key to this chapter. You can encourage children to experiment with:
- An italic style
- A note-taking style
- A speedy style
- Their best style (for display work, thank-you letters and so on)
- Other styles, such as a more rounded loop on 'y' and 'g' when joining or using different letter forms.

As part of developing an individual style, the children are also encouraged to experiment with the size of their writing, making it bigger or smaller by:
- Working on different-sized guidelines.
- Working on a range of different tasks, for example some things might require bigger writing rather than smaller writing.

Pangrams are also used (sentences that use every letter of the alphabet at least once). Time the children to see how long they take and then analyse the writing. Look for errors such as formation, size of overall writing and individual letter sizes (head, body, tail), slant and incorrect joins. Then repeat, trying to do it in a faster time with fewer errors. The aim is to build up speed but not let legibility disappear. High-frequency words can also provide practice for speed.

Punctuation is also looked at specifically within this chapter. Finally, a writing task section brings together all the handwriting knowledge the children have learned in order to complete an extended piece of writing.

In this chapter

Changing the size page 108	To practise handwriting using different sizes of script.
Developing your own style page 112	To explore different styles of handwriting and develop an individual style.
Punctuation page 116	To practise using accurate punctuation.
Practising speed page 120	To practise writing quickly, fluently and legibly.
Writing tasks page 124	To practise handwriting for different purposes.

Chapter 5

Changing the size

Objective

To practise handwriting using different sizes of script.

Background knowledge

People change the size of their writing for different purposes or occasions. Writing size is usually determined by the desired effect. For example, the size of a child's writing will be different when writing a formal letter or an essay to writing an advertisement or on a sticky note. Some children may find they lose fluency when increasing or decreasing the size of their writing or use a more printed style.

In this section, the children practise changing the size of their writing for different purposes. They use guidelines of reducing sizes and increasing sizes to experiment with the size of writing. They also write an advertisement poster and compare how the size of script affects the outcome. Finally, they practise writing tricky spellings using different sizes.

Left-handers may wish to lift their pen from the paper while joining, thus avoiding having to push awkwardly across the page. If the ink or pencil trace disappears, do not tell them they have to produce a joining mark. However, do ensure they are joining just above the paper, rather than printing. Left-handers may also want to produce a sharper, more italic-style exit to their end-low joins. This is fine as long as they leave enough space between their words and don't cramp their letters together.

Activities

● **Photocopiable page 109 'Big to small, small to big'**
The children practise changing the size of their writing by copying two proverbs into graduated guidelines, first starting large and getting smaller and then the reverse. They then write a sentence to say which they prefer, large writing or small writing.

● **Photocopiable page 110 'Advertising'**
In this activity, children copy a poster advertising a 'Victorian Fayre' and experiment with using different sizes of writing for different parts of the poster. Discuss the importance of the information on the poster, such as the date, and how they can emphasise this and make it eye-catching. Then the children explain their choices in a sentence.

● **Photocopiable page 111 'Tricky spellings'**
In this activity, children practise changing the size of their handwriting while also practising writing words with tricky spellings. They copy the words into boxes that gradually increase in size.

Further ideas

● **Monster and miniature:** Ask the children to produce a paragraph of 'monster writing' and then the same paragraph as 'miniature writing' and compare how the size affects their handwriting.
● **Curriculum sizes:** Encourage the children to experiment with the size of their writing while writing in other curriculum areas.
● **Plain paper:** Encourage the children to repeat the activities in this section using plain paper instead of lined paper.

What's on the CD-ROM

On the CD-ROM you will find:
● Graduated guidelines for 'Big to small, small to big'.
● Tramline practice areas for all three activities.
● All of the photocopiable sheets.

Scholastic Literacy Skills
Handwriting: Years 5–6

Name: Chapter 5

Changing the size

Big to small, small to big

■ Practise changing the size of your writing. Copy these proverbs into the guidelines.

1. A good beginning makes a good ending.

2. Birds of a feather flock together.

■ Write a sentence to say whether you prefer writing with larger letters or smaller letters, and why.

PHOTOCOPIABLE

Scholastic Literacy Skills
Handwriting: Years 5–6

Chapter 5

Name:

Changing the size

Advertising

■ Copy this poster and try out different sizes of writing for different sections to see which works best. Then write up the best version on a piece of plain paper and write a sentence to explain why you chose those sizes.

> Victorian Fayre
> Saturday March 12
> Lots of stalls
> Street entertainers
> Freshly prepared refreshments
> Bring the family
> 11am to 5pm

■ What makes this your best version?

_____

Scholastic Literacy Skills
Handwriting: Years 5–6

110

PHOTOCOPIABLE

SCHOLASTIC
www.scholastic.co.uk

Name:

Chapter 5

Changing the size

Tricky spellings

■ Practise changing the size of your writing. Write these tricky words in the present boxes. Remember to fit your writing to the size of the box.

| synonym | conscience | potential | embarrassment |
| rehearsal | committee | accommodation | government |

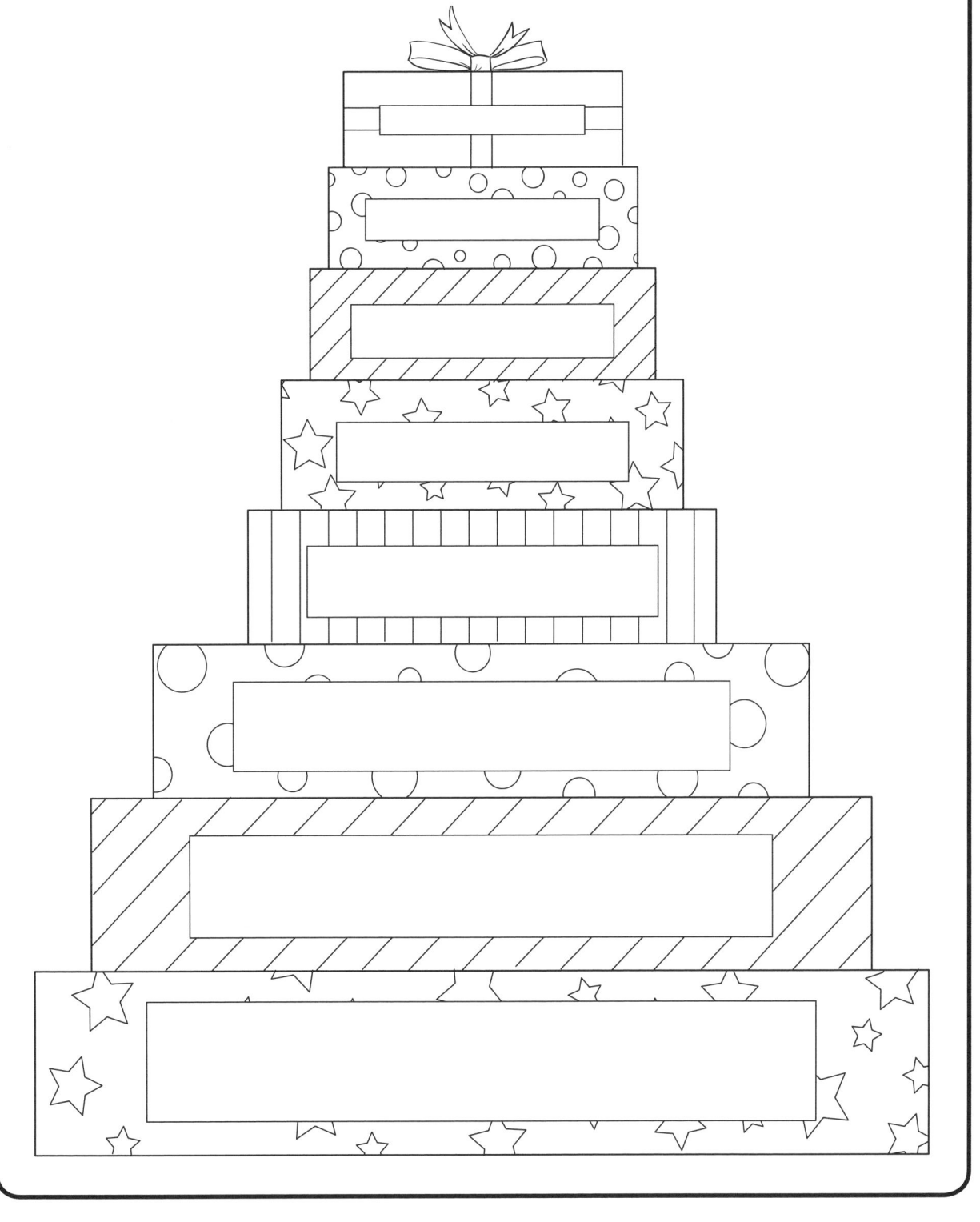

PHOTOCOPIABLE

Scholastic Literacy Skills
Handwriting: Years 5–6

www.scholastic.co.uk

111

Chapter 5

Developing your own style

Objective

To explore different styles of handwriting and develop an individual style.

Background knowledge

Different writing styles are used for different purposes and audiences. For example, a note or letter to a best friend would be different from a job application or an informative poster. Handwriting also doesn't have to always look beautiful. For example, when note taking, the audience is usually yourself so legibility is more important than appearance.

Everyone's handwriting is different. Even when children have been taught to use the same style, they develop individual differences in their writing. Having a clear but attractive handwriting style can make a good impression on the reader. The shape, slant and spacing of the letters all affect the style of writing, as does the type of writing implement used.

Left-handers may wish to lift their pen from the paper while joining, thus avoiding having to push awkwardly across the page. If the ink or pencil trace disappears, do not tell them they have to produce a joining mark. However, do ensure they are joining just above the paper, rather than printing. Left-handers may also want to produce a sharper, more italic-style exit to their end-low joins. This is fine as long as they leave enough space between their words and don't cramp their letters together.

Activities

● **Photocopiable page 113 'Using straight-edged pens'**
Provide the children with italic-style pens or felt-tipped calligraphy pens. Encourage them to write the poem provided (anonymous author), keeping the nib or tip of the pen at the same angle, developing a style with thin and thick strokes.

● **Photocopiable page 114 'Going loopy'**
In this activity, children copy a letter and experiment with adding more loops to their writing, particularly on the ascenders. However, it is important to note that lots of loops may cause some children to tire when writing longer pieces of work as their hand may not get a chance to rest. Make sure you stress to the children that this exercise is merely to introduce them to different ways of writing in order to experiment.

● **Photocopiable page 115 'Decorative writing'**
In this activity, children are encouraged to use a decorative writing style to copy a poem by Christina Rossetti. The task focuses specifically on adding decoration to capital letters. You may wish to find some examples of decorated capitals in books to show the children different examples.

Further ideas

● **Writing styles:** Children experiment with different writing styles, swap with a friend and compare the effects, describing good and bad aspects of the handwriting.
● **Style wall:** Create a style wall and encourage the children to add different handwriting styles, decorated poems and other effective examples.
● **Illuminating:** Encourage the children to create illuminated manuscripts using paint or other materials to decorate their writing.

What's on the CD-ROM

On the CD-ROM you will find:
● Animation of the joins.
● All of the photocopiable pages.

Name: Chapter 5

Developing your own style

Using straight-edged pens

■ Use a straight-edged nib or felt-tipped calligraphy pen to write this poem about spelling and pronunciation.

■ Keep the angle of your pen the same as you write to give thick and thin strokes.

> Beware of heard, a dreadful word
> That looks like beard and sounds like bird
> And dead – it's said like bed, not bead.
> For goodness' sake, don't call it deed!
> Watch out for meat and great and threat:
> They rhyme with suite and straight and debt.

■ Write it here.

_____
_____
_____
_____
_____
_____

■ Now try a different type of pen and write it again.

_____
_____
_____
_____
_____
_____

■ Which looks better? Give the one you prefer a tick.

Chapter 5 Name:

Developing your own style

Going loopy

- Some people use loops when they write ascenders, for example *muddle*
- Copy this letter and experiment with writing using loops in your handwriting.

Dear Grandma

I hope you are well.

Thank you for my birthday present. How did you know I wanted a football? It is great.

I have put it in my bedroom next to the ones you sent me last year and at Christmas. I now have a great collection of footballs. In fact, I think I've got more footballs than a football club!

I had a lovely birthday party but it was a shame you had to miss it.

I'm off to play football now. I got in the school team, so must finish writing.

I hope to see you again soon.

With love

Your grandson

Joe

Developing your own style

Decorative writing

■ Sometimes you might want to present your writing using a decorative writing style. This can be done by adding extra swirls to capital letters

■ Many decorated examples of writing add drawings and colour to the capitals at the start of a paragraph, or make the capital letter much bigger than the rest of the text.

■ Copy this poem and use decorated capital letters to make it look attractive.

Who has seen the wind?
Neither I nor you:
But when the leaves hang trembling,
The wind is passing through.
Who has seen the wind?
Neither you nor I:
But when the trees bow down their heads,
The wind is passing by.

Christina Rossetti

Chapter 5

Punctuation

Objective

To practise using accurate punctuation.

Background knowledge

Punctuation is important in writing as it helps make the meaning clear for readers, and helps them to read with expression.

The bottom of most punctuation marks sits on the writing line (level with the bottom of an 'a'). Care should be taken to ensure they aren't positioned too high or too low, or they can be mistaken for other punctuation and cause confusion. For example, placing a comma or a full stop too high might mean it looks like an apostrophe. Care should be taken with the top parts of exclamation and question marks so that they do not join with the dot.

Speech marks are placed level with the top of the capital letter, both at the beginning and at the end of the spoken words. Care should be taken that the speech mark at the end of the spoken words isn't placed too low, especially when the last letter has no ascender. Children should also be made aware that the speech marks are placed outside of other punctuation (after the full stop, exclamation mark or question mark).

More unusual punctuation includes the colon and hyphen. Emphasis should be given to making sure the marks for a colon are placed directly above and below each other or they won't give the reader the correct information about the sentence. A colon is used to indicate that a list will follow or that a new idea will be introduced.

Children should be taught when to use a hyphen, and its position just above the baseline. Hyphens are used to join two words for an adjective ('that is very off-putting'), for certain compound words, or whenever 'self' is used ('self-expression', 'self-control'). They can also be used to avoid ambiguity. For example, 'a long standing friend' is different from 'a long-standing friend'.

Activities

- **Photocopiable page 117 'Revising common punctuation'**
This activity revises common punctuation marks as the children copy a punctuated paragraph that is the beginning of a story. It contains speech marks, commas, full stops, apostrophes, question marks and exclamation marks. They then rewrite the next paragraph and add the missing punctuation.
- **Photocopiable page 118 'Practice with colons'**
Before completing the activity, remind or explain to the children that a colon comes before a list, and the list components are separated by commas. Ask the children to read the three sentences each time, identify the one that uses the colon correctly and copy it.
- **Photocopiable page 119 'Fun with hyphens'**
In this activity, children choose the correct use of hyphens in pairs of sentences. In one sentence out of the two, the lack of the hyphen gives the sentence an ambiguous meaning. A question follows the two sentences to give the children a clue.

Further ideas

- **Punctuation partners:** Encourage the children to write a paragraph without any punctuation, swap it with a partner and ask them to punctuate it.
- **Unusual punctuation:** Encourage the children to collect examples of less-familiar punctuation usage in reading and in other curriculum areas, for example hyphenated numbers in numeracy.

What's on the CD-ROM

On the CD-ROM you will find:
- Annotate the punctuation on screen for all three activities.
- Tramline practice areas for all three activities.
- All of the photocopiable pages.

Punctuation

Revising common punctuation

■ The most common punctuation marks are:

full stop	.	speech marks	" "
comma	,	question mark	?
apostrophe	'	exclamation mark	!

■ Copy the start of the story carefully. Notice all the punctuation marks.

Saira and her mum went shopping for new shoes.
"Oh look at those!" cried Saira. "They're lovely."
"Oh Saira," said Mum. "We need school shoes. Pink ones won't do at all."
"They've got them in blue. Can I have those?" asked Saira.

_____

_____

_____

_____

_____

■ Now rewrite the next part of the story. Add all the missing punctuation marks.

Mum looked at the blue shoes
They are nice she agreed but you need black ones for school
Can you ask the lady if they have them in black asked Saira
That's a good idea said Mum and went to find an assistant

_____

_____

_____

_____

Chapter 5   Name:

Punctuation

Practice with colons

- A colon is used to show a list will follow a statement.
- Read the three sentences and copy the one with the correct punctuation.

1. Year 6 pupils should bring the following, wellingtons: wet weather clothes, indoor shoes and warm sweaters.

   Year 6 pupils should bring the following: wellingtons, wet weather clothes, indoor shoes and warm sweaters.

   Year 6 pupils should bring the following, wellingtons, wet weather clothes, indoor shoes and warm sweaters:

   _____

   _____

2. At the Fun Farm you can see: pigs and piglets, sheep and lambs, cows and calves, chickens and geese.

   At the Fun Farm: you can see pigs and piglets, sheep and lambs, cows and calves, chickens and geese.

   At the Fun Farm you can see pigs and piglets: sheep and lambs: cows and calves: chicken and geese.

   _____

   _____

3. We have only two rules and they are: these, always be polite and tidy up after yourself.

   We have only two rules and they are these: always be polite and tidy up after yourself.

   We only have two rules and they are these, always be polite: and tidy up after yourself.

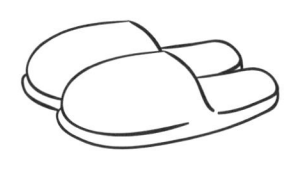

   _____

   _____

118 Scholastic Literacy Skills
     Handwriting: Years 5–6

Punctuation

Fun with hyphens

■ Which one of these pairs of sentences makes sense? The questions give you a clue.
■ Copy the correct one.

1. Mum bought some fabric to recover the sofa.
   Mum bought some fabric to re-cover the sofa.
   Is the sofa ill?

   _____

2. We saw a dark haired lady in the café.
   We saw a dark-haired lady in the café.
   Was the lady dark or was it her hair?

   _____

3. The book is by a well known writer.
   The book is by a well-known writer.
   Is the writer in good health or famous?

   _____

4. She didn't get my letter so I re-sent it.
   She didn't get my letter so I resent it.
   What does 'resent' mean?

   _____

5. A man eating shark has been seen off the coast.
   A man-eating shark has been seen off the coast.
   Was the man eating the shark?

   _____

6. Spiders are eight legged creepy-crawlies.
   Spiders are eight-legged creepy-crawlies.
   How many creepy-crawlies?

   _____

Practising speed

Objective

To practise writing quickly, fluently and legibly.

Background knowledge

Children need to develop a fluent, legible and speedy script in order to be able to write quickly. Note that the average writing speed for children aged 9 is 38 letters per minute, aged 10 is 46 letters per minute and aged 11 is 52 letters per minute.

Pangrams are useful for developing this skill as they are sentences that use every letter of the alphabet at least once. Use one pangram a week and ask the children to write one out each day and time it. Once complete, the handwriting should be analysed using the photocopiable page 123 'Handwriting checklist'. Then repeat the exercise, encouraging them to do it in a faster time, but with more ticks in the checklist. The aim is to build up speed but not let legibility decrease. If a persistent mistake appears, then the child needs some revision – it could be a letter form, join or so on. They should return to guideline paper to consolidate before returning once more to lined paper.

High-frequency words can also provide practice for speed. As an aid to building up speed, the children can experiment with slanting their handwriting more to the right or left, or not at all.

Left-handers may wish to lift their pen from the paper while joining, thus avoiding having to push awkwardly across the page. If the ink or pencil trace disappears, do not tell them they have to produce a joining mark. However, do ensure they are joining just above the paper, rather than printing. Left-handers may also want to produce a sharper, more italic-style exit to their end-low joins. This is fine as long as they leave enough space between their words and don't cramp their letters together.

Activities

- **Photocopiable page 121 'Pangrams'**
The children are given six pangrams. They choose one and time how long it takes them to copy it. They can then repeat the activity every day for a week to build up speed and fluency. Encourage them to use photocopiable page 123 'Handwriting checklist' to check their accuracy. They can choose another, different pangram to practise with in the following weeks.
- **Photocopiable page 122 'Six shorter pangrams'**
In this activity, the children are given six shorter pangrams to copy and time individually. They can then repeat the activity several times to build up speed and fluency. Encourage them to use photocopiable page 123 'Handwriting checklist' to check their accuracy.
- **Photocopiable page 123 'Handwriting checklist'**
This page provides a checklist so the children can assess all the aspects of their own handwriting. Encourage them to use it regularly, and in particular when building up the speed of their writing.

Further ideas

- **Rewriting:** Using poetry, rhymes and their own writing, encourage the children to re-write a text several times and try to build up their speed while not losing legibility.
- **Against the clock:** Hold 'against the clock' writing sessions. Display a paragraph from a familiar text on the board and give the children a limited time in which to write it. Then ask them to use photocopiable page 123 'Handwriting checklist' to check their handwriting.
- **Musical:** Ask the children to write to music. Experiment with fast and slow rhythmical music.

What's on the CD-ROM

On the CD-ROM you will find:
- Tramline practice areas for all three activities.
- All of the photocopiable pages.

Name: Chapter 5

Practising speed

Pangrams

■ These sentences are called pangrams. They use every letter of the alphabet.
■ Choose one pangram to copy as quickly as you can and time yourself. Then repeat it every day for a week and see how fast you can get.
■ The next week, choose a different pangram and copy it every day, timing yourself.
■ Continue with the remaining pangrams.

Time

1. Six big juicy steaks sizzled in a pan as five workmen left the quarry.

   _____

2. While making deep excavations we found some quaint bronze jewellery.

   _____

3. Jaded zombies acted quaintly but kept driving their oxen forward.

   _____

4. A mad boxer shot a quick, gloved jab to the jaw of his dizzy opponent.

   _____

5. The job requires extra pluck and zeal from every young wage earner.

   _____

6. A quart jar of oil mixed with zinc oxide makes a very bright paint.

   _____

SCHOLASTIC   PHOTOCOPIABLE   Scholastic Literacy Skills
www.scholastic.co.uk   Handwriting: Years 5–6   121

Chapter 5   Name:

Practising speed

Six shorter pangrams

■ Copy these shorter pangrams. How fast can you write each one and still be legible and neat?

Time

1. Amazingly few discotheques provide jukeboxes.
_____

2. Heavy boxes perform quick waltzes and jigs.
_____

3. Jinxed wizards pluck ivy from the big quilt.
_____

4. The quick brown fox jumps over a lazy dog.
_____

5. Pack my box with five dozen liquor jugs.
_____

6. The five boxing wizards jump quickly.
_____

Name: Chapter 5

Practising speed

Handwriting checklist

■ Here is a useful list to help you check your handwriting.

Size
Is the writing a good size for the page and width of lines? ☐
Are the letters the correct size? ☐
Do the letters hit the top or bottom of the body, head and tail line correctly? ☐

Shape
Are the letters the correct shapes?
- Straight down – 'i', 'j', 'l', 't', 'u', 'y' ☐
- Down, up and over – 'b', 'h', 'k', 'm', 'n', 'p', 'r' ☐
- Up, backwards and around – 'a', 'c', 'd', 'e', 'f', 'g', 'o', 'q', 's' ☐
- Zooming – 'v', 'w', 'x', 'z' ☐

Position
Are the letters sitting on the writing line? ☐

Word and letter spaces
Are the spaces correct?
- Between words ☐
- Between letters ☐

Slant
Is the writing slanting in the same direction? ☐

Joining
Is the writing joined correctly? ☐

Speed
Was the writing written fast enough? ☐
Can it still be read? ☐

Legibility
Are any mistakes crossed out neatly? ☐

SCHOLASTIC   PHOTOCOPIABLE
www.scholastic.co.uk

Scholastic Literacy Skills
Handwriting: Years 5–6   123

Chapter 5

Writing tasks

Objective

To practise handwriting for different purposes.

Background knowledge

Understanding the purpose and audience for writing is key to producing effective texts. When the children are given writing tasks for different purposes and audiences, they can practise their handwriting in the context of real-life writing rather than just for the specific purpose of practice. As they develop their own style within the context of different text types and audiences, they need to keep in mind the importance of legibility.

Children need to make sure that ascenders and descenders don't touch the lines above and below, thereby reducing legibility. Children need to use their judgement about how to space out their writing so ascenders and descenders don't hit each other.

Left-handers may wish to lift their pen from the paper while joining, thus avoiding having to push awkwardly across the page. If the ink or pencil trace disappears, do not tell them they have to produce a joining mark. However, do ensure they are joining just above the paper, rather than printing. Left-handers may also want to produce a sharper, more italic-style exit. This is fine as long as they leave enough space between their words and don't cramp their letters together.

Encourage the children to analyse their extended writing pieces using photocopiable page 123 'Handwriting checklist'.

Activities

- **Photocopiable page 125 'Stories'**
In this activity, children practise handwriting during the longer task of planning and writing a story. The photocopiable sheet provides a chart of ideas with space for them to add notes of ideas based on setting, character, plot, style and dialogue. They then write the story on plain paper.
- **Photocopiable page 126 'Non-fiction'**
The children practise handwriting while writing an explanation of the water cycle. Prior to starting the activity, remind the children of the typical features and language used in explanation texts. Show the children the diagram and talk it through with them, discuss where the explanation should begin, and collect words and phrases that would be useful for the explanation, such as technical terms and connectives to show the sequence.
- **Photocopiable page 127 'Informal non-fiction'**
In this activity, children write a diary entry about an imaginary talent contest they had entered. Before beginning to write, encourage the children to talk about the sort of things that happen on talent shows, and how the contestants feel before, during and after such contests. Explain that the audience for a diary is themselves, so they can use writing and language in an informal way to suit their own personalities.

Further ideas

- **Poster:** Encourage the children to write posters for school events such as fetes, author or drama visits, school trips and clubs.
- **Captions:** Encourage the children to write captions and labels for class displays rather than using printed or computer-generated ones.
- **Letters:** Encourage the children to write letters to real people, for example their favourite pop star, a thank-you letter to their favourite lunchtime supervisor and so on.

What's on the CD-ROM

On the CD-ROM you will find:
- Tramline practice areas for all three activities.
- All of the photocopiable pages.

Name: Chapter 5

Writing tasks

Stories

■ Write a story to practise your handwriting. Use the sections in the story planner below to get ideas. Then write your story on plain paper.

Setting Where is the story set? *Some ideas:* a housing estate, a mysterious castle, a ship, a jungle, the seaside *Your notes:*	**Characters** Who is in your story? *Some ideas:* Heroes: a boy or a girl or both, a wise old man, a superhero, an animal Villains: a gangster, a witch or wizard, a superhero, pirates *Your notes:*
Plot What happens in your story? *Some ideas:* something gets lost or stolen, something strange is discovered, someone is given a difficult task *Your notes:*	**Style** What sort of story will it be? *Some ideas:* mystery, adventure, fantasy, myth, legend, traditional tale, fairy tale *Your notes:*
Structure How does your story start? How does it end? *Your notes:*	**Dialogue and good words** Note down some ideas of good words and dialogue for your characters and plot:

SCHOLASTIC
www.scholastic.co.uk   **PHOTOCOPIABLE**

Scholastic Literacy Skills
Handwriting: Years 5–6

Chapter 5　　　　　　　Name:

Writing tasks

Non-fiction

- Write an explanation of the water cycle for younger children.
- Use the diagram to help you.

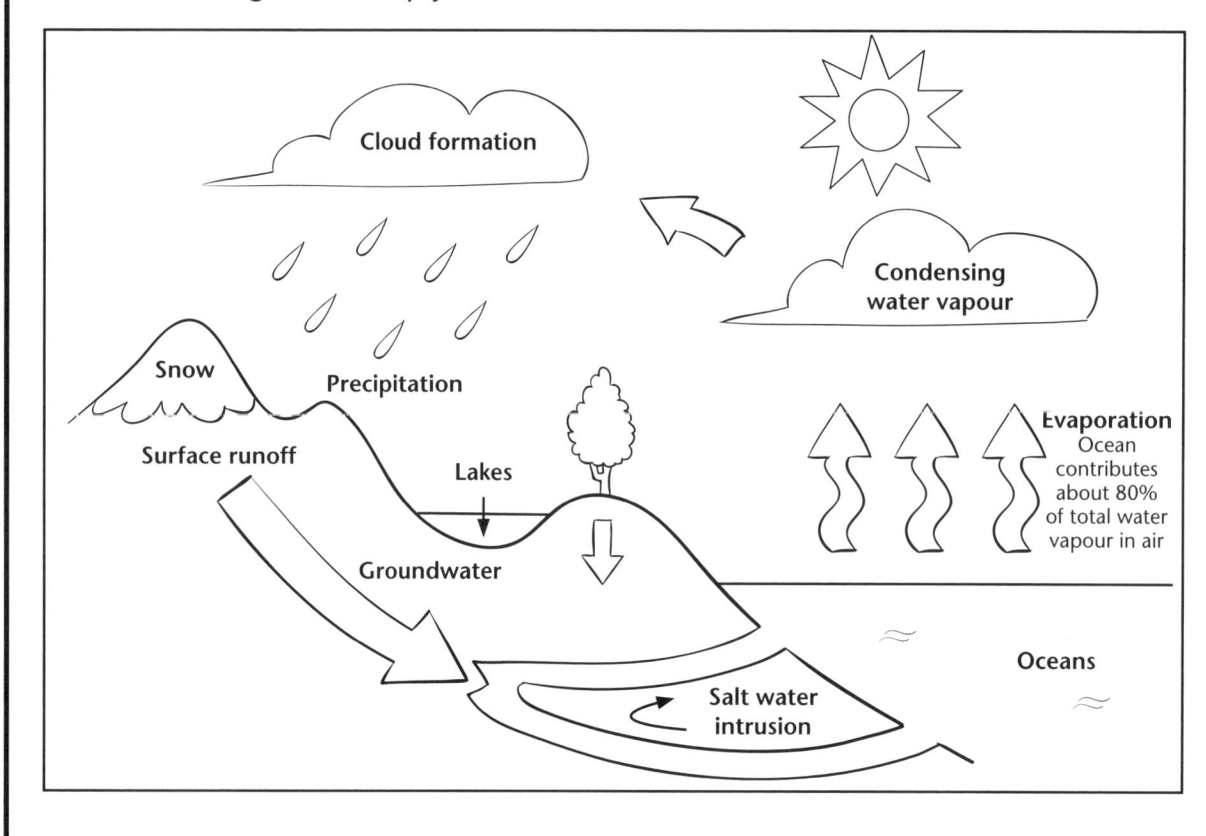

Cloud formation

Condensing water vapour

Snow　**Precipitation**

Surface runoff　**Lakes**

Groundwater

Evaporation
Ocean contributes about 80% of total water vapour in air

Salt water intrusion

Oceans

_____

_____

_____

_____

_____

_____

_____

_____

Scholastic Literacy Skills　　　　　　　　　　　　PHOTOCOPIABLE
126　Handwriting: Years 5–6　　　　　　　　　　　　www.scholastic.co.uk

Name:

Chapter 5

Writing tasks

Informal non-fiction

■ Imagine you have been a contestant on a talent show. Write a diary entry to describe your day, how it built up to your turn to perform, what happened and, importantly, how you felt about it all.

■ Remember, you are the audience for your writing, so you can be casual, humorous or serious.

■ Use the beginning to start you off.

Dear Diary
Today was the BIG day!

SCHOLASTIC

Also available in this series:

ISBN 978-1407-12787-3    ISBN 978-1407-12788-0    ISBN 978-1407-12789-7

Grammar and punctuation

Years 1–2	ISBN 978-1407-10045-6
Year 3	ISBN 978-1407-10046-3
Year 4	ISBN 978-1407-10047-0
Year 5	ISBN 978-1407-10048-7
Year 6	ISBN 978-1407-10049-4

Spelling

Years 1–2	ISBN 978-1407-10055-5
Year 3	ISBN 978-1407-10056-2
Year 4	ISBN 978-1407-10057-9
Year 5	ISBN 978-1407-10058-6
Year 6	ISBN 978-1407-10059-3

Comprehension

Years 1–2	ISBN 978-1407-10050-0
Year 3	ISBN 978-1407-10051-7
Year 4	ISBN 978-1407-10052-4
Year 5	ISBN 978-1407-10053-1
Year 6	ISBN 978-1407-10054-8

Vocabulary

Years 1–2	ISBN 978-1407-10223-8
Year 3	ISBN 978-1407-10224-5
Year 4	ISBN 978-1407-10225-2
Year 5	ISBN 978-1407-10226-9
Year 6	ISBN 978-1407-10227-6

To find out more, call: 0845 603 9091
or visit our website www.scholastic.co.uk